FOREWORD

The collection of "Everything Will Be Okay" travel phrasebooks published by T&P Books is designed for people traveling abroad for tourism and business. The phrasebooks contain what matters most - the essentials for basic communication. This is an indispensable set of phrases to "survive" while abroad.

This phrasebook will help you in most cases where you need to ask something, get directions, find out how much something costs, etc. It can also resolve difficult communication situations where gestures just won't help.

This book contains a lot of phrases that have been grouped according to the most relevant topics. The edition also includes a small vocabulary that contains roughly 3,000 of the most frequently used words. Another section of the phrasebook provides a gastronomical dictionary that may help you order food at a restaurant or buy groceries at the store.

Take "Everything Will Be Okay" phrasebook with you on the road and you'll have an irreplaceable traveling companion who will help you find your way out of any situation and teach you to not fear speaking with foreigners.

TABLE OF CONTENTS

T&P Books Publishing

PRONUNCIATION

Letter	Korean example	T&P phonetic alphabet	English example

Consonants

Letter	Korean example	T&P phonetic alphabet	English example
ㄱ [1]	개	[k]	clock, kiss
ㄱ [2]	아기	[g]	game, gold
ㄲ	껌	[k]	tense [k]
ㄴ	눈	[n]	name, normal
ㄷ [3]	달	[t]	tourist, trip
ㄷ [4]	사다리	[d]	day, doctor
ㄸ	딸	[t]	tense [t]
ㄹ [5]	라디오	[r]	rice, radio
ㄹ [6]	십팔	[l]	lace, people
ㅁ	문	[m]	magic, milk
ㅂ [7]	봄	[p]	pencil, private
ㅂ [8]	아버지	[b]	baby, book
ㅃ	빵	[p]	tense [p]
ㅅ [9]	실	[s]	city, boss
ㅅ [10]	옷	[t]	tourist, trip
ㅆ	쌀	[ja:]	royal
ㅇ [11]	강	[ŋg]	language, single
ㅈ [12]	집	[tɕ]	cheer
ㅈ [13]	아주	[dʑ]	jeans, gene
ㅉ	짬	[tɕ]	tense [tch]
ㅊ	차	[tɕh]	hitchhiker
ㅌ	택시	[th]	don't have
ㅋ	칼	[kh]	work hard
ㅍ	포도	[ph]	top hat
ㅎ	한국	[h]	home, have

Letter	Korean example	T&P phonetic alphabet	English example

Vowels and combinations with vowels

Letter	Korean example	T&P phonetic alphabet	English example
ㅏ	사	[a]	shorter than in ask
ㅑ	향	[ja]	Kenya, piano
ㅓ	머리	[ʌ]	lucky, sun
ㅕ	병	[jɑ]	young, yard
ㅗ	몸	[o]	pod, John
ㅛ	표	[jɔ]	New York
ㅜ	꿀	[u]	book
ㅠ	슈퍼	[ju]	youth, usually
ㅡ	음악	[ɪ]	big, America
ㅣ	길	[i], [iː]	feet, Peter
ㅐ	뺌	[ɛ], [ɛː]	habit, bad
ㅒ	얘기	[je]	yesterday, yen
ㅔ	펜	[e]	elm, medal
ㅖ	계산	[je]	yesterday, yen
ㅘ	왕	[wa]	watt, white
ㅙ	왜	[ʊə]	pure, fuel
ㅚ	회의	[ø], [we]	first, web
ㅝ	권	[ʊɔ]	to order, to open
ㅞ	웬	[ʊə]	pure, fuel
ㅟ	쥐	[wi]	whiskey
ㅢ	거의	[ɰi]	combination [ɪi]

Comments

1 at the beginning of words
2 between voiced sounds
3 at the beginning of words
4 between voiced sounds
5 at the beginning of a syllable
6 at the end of a syllable
7 at the beginning of words
8 between voiced sounds
9 at the beginning of a syllable
10 at the end of a syllable
11 at the end of a syllable
12 at the beginning of words
13 between voiced sounds

LIST OF ABBREVIATIONS

English abbreviations

ab.	-	about
adj	-	adjective
adv	-	adverb
anim.	-	animate
as adj	-	attributive noun used as adjective
e.g.	-	for example
etc.	-	et cetera
fam.	-	familiar
fem.	-	feminine
form.	-	formal
inanim.	-	inanimate
masc.	-	masculine
math	-	mathematics
mil.	-	military
n	-	noun
pl	-	plural
pron.	-	pronoun
sb	-	somebody
sing.	-	singular
sth	-	something
v aux	-	auxiliary verb
vi	-	intransitive verb
vi, vt	-	intransitive, transitive verb
vt	-	transitive verb

KOREAN
PHRASEBOOK

This section contains
important phrases that may
come in handy in various
real-life situations.
The phrasebook will help
you ask for directions, clarify
a price, buy tickets, and
order food at a restaurant

T&P Books Publishing

PHRASEBOOK
CONTENTS

T&P Books Publishing

The bare minimum

Excuse me, ...
실례합니다, …
sil-lye-ham-ni-da, ...

Hello.
안녕하세요.
an-nyeong-ha-se-yo.

Thank you.
감사합니다.
gam-sa-ham-ni-da.

Good bye.
안녕히 계세요.
an-nyeong-hi gye-se-yo.

Yes.
네.
ne.

No.
아니오.
a-ni-o.

I don't know.
모르겠어요.
mo-reu-ge-seo-yo.

Where? | Where to? | When?
어디예요? | 어디까지 가세요? |
언제요?
eo-di-ye-yo? | eo-di-kka-ji ga-se-yo? |
eon-je-yo?

I need ...
… 필요해요.
… pi-ryo-hae-yo.

I want ...
… 싶어요.
… si-peo-yo.

Do you have ...?
… 있으세요?
… i-seu-se-yo?

Is there a ... here?
여기 … 있어요?
yeo-gi … i-seo-yo?

May I ...?
…해도 되나요?
… hae-do doe-na-yo?

..., please (polite request)
…, 부탁합니다.
…, bu-tak-am-ni-da.

I'm looking for ...
… 찾고 있어요.
… chat-go i-seo-yo.

restroom
화장실
hwa-jang-sil

ATM
현금인출기
hyeon-geum-in-chul-gi

pharmacy (drugstore)
약국
yak-guk

hospital
병원
byeong-won

police station
경찰서
gyeong-chal-seo

subway	지하철 ji-ha-cheol
taxi	택시 taek-si
train station	기차역 gi-cha-yeok

My name is ...	제 이름은 … 입니다. je i-reu-meun ... im-ni-da.
What's your name?	성함이 어떻게 되세요? seong-ham-i eo-tteo-ke doe-se-yo?
Could you please help me?	도와주세요. do-wa-ju-se-yo.
I've got a problem.	문제가 있어요. mun-je-ga i-seo-yo.
I don't feel well.	몸이 안 좋아요. mom-i an jo-a-yo.
Call an ambulance!	구급차를 불러 주세요! gu-geup-cha-reul bul-leo ju-se-yo!
May I make a call?	전화를 써도 되나요? jeon-hwa-reul sseo-do doe-na-yo?

I'm sorry.	죄송합니다. joe-song-ham-ni-da.
You're welcome.	천만에요. cheon-man-e-yo.

I, me	저 jeo
you (inform.)	너 neo
he	그 geu
she	그녀 geu-nyeo
they (masc.)	그들 geu-deul
they (fem.)	그들 geu-deul
we	우리 u-ri
you (pl)	너희 neo-hui
you (sg, form.)	당신 dang-sin

ENTRANCE	입구 ip-gu
EXIT	출구 chul-gu
OUT OF ORDER	고장 go-jang

CLOSED	**닫힘** da-chim
OPEN	**열림** yeol-lim
FOR WOMEN	**여성용** yeo-seong-yong
FOR MEN	**남성용** nam-seong-yong

Questions

Where?	어디예요? eo-di-ye-yo?
Where to?	어디까지 가세요? eo-di-kka-ji ga-se-yo?
Where from?	어디에서요? eo-di-e-seo-yo?
Why?	왜요? wae-yo?
For what reason?	무슨 이유에서요? mu-seun i-yu-e-seo-yo?
When?	언제요? eon-je-yo?
How long?	얼마나요? eol-ma-na-yo?
At what time?	몇 시에요? myeot si-e-yo?
How much?	얼마예요? eol-ma-ye-yo?
Do you have ...?	··· 있으세요? ... i-seu-se-yo?
Where is ...?	··· 어디 있어요? ... eo-di i-seo-yo?
What time is it?	지금 몇 시예요? ji-geum myeot si-ye-yo?
May I make a call?	전화를 써도 되나요? jeon-hwa-reul sseo-do doe-na-yo?
Who's there?	누구세요? nu-gu-se-yo?
Can I smoke here?	담배를 피워도 되나요? dam-bae-reul pi-wo-do doe-na-yo?
May I ...?	··· 되나요? ... doe-na-yo?

Needs

I'd like ...	··· 하고 싶어요. ... ha-go si-peo-yo.
I don't want ...	··· 하기 싫어요. ... ha-gi si-reo-yo.
I'm thirsty.	목이 말라요. mo-gi mal-la-yo.
I want to sleep.	자고 싶어요. ja-go si-peo-yo,
I want ...	··· 싶어요. ... si-peo-yo.
to wash up	씻고 ssit-go
to brush my teeth	이를 닦고 i-reul dak-go
to rest a while	쉬고 swi-go
to change my clothes	옷을 갈아입고 os-eul ga-ra-ip-go
to go back to the hotel	호텔로 돌아가고 ho-tel-lo do-ra-ga-go
to buy ...	··· 사고 ... sa-go
to go to ...	···에 가고 ...e ga-go
to visit ...	···에 방문하고 ...e bang-mun-ha-go
to meet with ...	··· 만나고 ... man-na-go
to make a call	전화를 걸고 jeon-hwa-reul geol-go
I'm tired.	저는 지쳤어요. jeo-neun ji-chyeo-seo-yo.
We are tired.	우리는 지쳤어요. u-ri-neun ji-chyeo-seo-yo.
I'm cold.	추워요. chu-wo-yo.
I'm hot.	더워요. deo-wo-yo.
I'm OK.	괜찮아요. gwaen-cha-na-yo.

16

I need to make a call.

전화를 걸어야 해요.
jeon-hwa-reul geo-reo-ya hae-yo.

I need to go to the restroom.

화장실에 가야 해요.
hwa-jang-si-re ga-ya hae-yo.

I have to go.

가야 해요.
ga-ya hae-yo.

I have to go now.

지금 가야 해요.
ji-geum ga-ya hae-yo.

Asking for directions

Excuse me, ...	실례합니다, ... sil-lye-ham-ni-da, ...
Where is ...?	... 어디 있어요? ... eo-di i-seo-yo?
Which way is ...?	... 어느 쪽이에요? ... eo-neu jjo-gi-ye-yo?
Could you help me, please?	도와주실 수 있어요? do-wa-ju-sil su i-seo-yo?

I'm looking for ...	... 찾고 있어요. ... chat-go i-seo-yo.
I'm looking for the exit.	출구를 찾고 있어요. chul-gu-reul chat-go i-seo-yo.
I'm going to ...	...에 가고 있어요. ... e ga-go i-seo-yo.
Am I going the right way to ...?	...에 가는데 이 길이 맞아요? ...e ga-neun-de i gi-ri ma-ja-yo?

Is it far?	먼가요? meon-ga-yo?
Can I get there on foot?	걸어갈 수 있어요? geo-reo-gal su i-seo-yo?
Can you show me on the map?	지도에서 보여주실 수 있어요? ji-do-e-seo bo-yeo-ju-sil su i-seo-yo?
Show me where we are right now.	지금 우리가 있는 곳을 보여주세요. ji-geum u-ri-ga in-neun gos-eul bo-yeo-ju-se-yo.

Here	여기 yeo-gi
There	거기 geo-gi
This way	이 길 i gil

Turn right.	오른쪽으로 가세요. o-reun-jjo-geu-ro ga-se-yo.
Turn left.	왼쪽으로 가세요. oen-jjo-geu-ro ga-se-yo.
first (second, third) turn	첫 번째 (두 번째, 세 번째) 골목 cheot beon-jjae (du beon-jjae, se beon-jjae) gol-mok

to the right	오른쪽으로
	o-reun-jjo-geu-ro
to the left	왼쪽으로
	oen-jjo-geu-ro
Go straight ahead.	직진하세요.
	jik-jin-ha-se-yo.

Signs

WELCOME!	**환영!** hwa-nyeong!
ENTRANCE	**입구** ip-gu
EXIT	**출구** chul-gu

PUSH	**미세요** mi-se-yo
PULL	**당기세요** dang-gi-se-yo
OPEN	**열림** yeol-lim
CLOSED	**닫힘** da-chim

FOR WOMEN	**여성용** yeo-seong-yong
FOR MEN	**남성용** nam-seong-yong
GENTLEMEN, GENTS (m)	**남성 (남)** nam-seong (nam)
WOMEN (f)	**여성 (여)** yeo-seong (yeo)

DISCOUNTS	**할인** ha-rin
SALE	**세일** se-il
FREE	**무료** mu-ryo
NEW!	**신상품!** sin-sang-pum!
ATTENTION!	**주의!** ju-ui!

NO VACANCIES	**빈 방 없음** bin bang eop-seum
RESERVED	**예약석** ye-yak-seok
ADMINISTRATION	**사무실** sa-mu-sil
STAFF ONLY	**직원 전용** ji-gwon jeo-nyong

BEWARE OF THE DOG! 개조심!
gae-jo-sim!

NO SMOKING! 금연!
geu-myeon!

DO NOT TOUCH! 만지지 마세요!
man-ji-ji ma-se-yo!

DANGEROUS 위험
wi-heom

DANGER 위험
wi-heom

HIGH VOLTAGE 고압 전류
go-ap jeol-lyu

NO SWIMMING! 수영금지!
su-yeong-geum-ji!

OUT OF ORDER 고장
go-jang

FLAMMABLE 가연성
ga-yeon-seong

FORBIDDEN 금지
geum-ji

NO TRESPASSING! 무단횡단 금지
mu-dan-hoeng-dan geum-ji

WET PAINT 젖은 페인트
jeo-jeun pe-in-teu

CLOSED FOR RENOVATIONS 공사중
gong-sa-jung

WORKS AHEAD 전방 공사중
jeon-bang gong-sa-jung

DETOUR 우회 도로
u-hoe do-ro

Transportation. General phrases

plane	비행기 bi-haeng-gi
train	기차 gi-cha
bus	버스 beo-seu
ferry	페리 pe-ri
taxi	택시 taek-si
car	자동차 ja-dong-cha

schedule	시간표 si-gan-pyo
Where can I see the schedule?	시간표는 어디서 볼 수 있어요? si-gan-pyo-neun eo-di-seo bol su i-seo-yo?

workdays (weekdays)	평일 pyeong-il
weekends	주말 ju-mal
holidays	휴일 hyu-il

DEPARTURE	출발 chul-bal
ARRIVAL	도착 do-chak
DELAYED	지연 ji-yeon
CANCELLED	취소 chwi-so

next (train, etc.)	다음 da-eum
first	첫 번째 cheot beon-jjae
last	마지막 ma-ji-mak

When is the next ...?

다음 … 언제인가요?
da-eum ... eon-je-in-ga-yo?

When is the first ...?

첫 … 언제인가요?
cheot ... eon-je-in-ga-yo?

When is the last ...?

마지막 … 언제인가요?
ma-ji-mak ... eon-je-in-ga-yo?

---

transfer (change of trains, etc.)

환승
hwan-seung

to make a transfer

환승하다
hwan-seung-ha-da

Do I need to make a transfer?

환승해야 해요?
hwan-seung-hae-ya hae-yo?

Buying tickets

Where can I buy tickets?	표는 어디서 사나요? pyo-neun eo-di-seo sa-na-yo?
ticket	표 pyo
to buy a ticket	표를 사다 pyo-reul sa-da
ticket price	표 가격 pyo ga-gyeok

Where to?	어디까지 가세요? eo-di-kka-ji ga-se-yo?
To what station?	어느 역까지 가세요? eo-neu yeok-kka-ji ga-se-yo?
I need ...	··· 필요해요. ... pi-ryo-hae-yo.
one ticket	표 한 장 pyo han jang
two tickets	표 두 장 pyo du jang
three tickets	표 세 장 pyo se jang

one-way	편도 pyeon-do
round-trip	왕복 wang-bok
first class	일등석 il-deung-seok
second class	이등석 i-deung-seok

today	오늘 o-neul
tomorrow	내일 nae-il
the day after tomorrow	모레 mo-re
in the morning	아침에 a-chim-e
in the afternoon	오후에 o-hu-e
in the evening	저녁에 jeo-nyeo-ge

aisle seat	복도 좌석 bok-do jwa-seok
window seat	창가 좌석 chang-ga jwa-seok
How much?	얼마예요? eol-ma-ye-yo?
Can I pay by credit card?	신용카드 돼요? si-nyong-ka-deu dwae-yo?

Bus

bus	버스 beo-seu
intercity bus	시외버스 si-oe-beo-seu
bus stop	버스 정류장 beo-seu jeong-nyu-jang
Where's the nearest bus stop?	가까운 버스 정류장이 어디예요? ga-kka-un beo-seu jeong-nyu-jang-i eo-di-ye-yo?

number (bus ~, etc.)	번호 beon-ho
Which bus do I take to get to …?	…에 가려면 어느 버스를 타야 해요? … e ga-ryeo-myeon eo-neu beo-seu-reul ta-ya hae-yo?
Does this bus go to …?	이 버스 … 가요? i beo-seu ... ga-yo?
How frequent are the buses?	버스는 얼마나 자주 와요? beo-seu-neun eol-ma-na ja-ju wa-yo?

every 15 minutes	십오 분 마다 si-bo bun ma-da
every half hour	삼십 분 마다 sam-sip bun ma-da
every hour	한 시간 마다 han si-gan ma-da
several times a day	하루에 여러 번 ha-ru-e yeo-reo beon
… times a day	하루에 …번 ha-ru-e ...beon

schedule	시간표 si-gan-pyo
Where can I see the schedule?	시간표는 어디서 볼 수 있어요? si-gan-pyo-neun eo-di-seo bol su i-seo-yo?
When is the next bus?	다음 버스는 언제인가요? da-eum beo-seu-neun eon-je-in-ga-yo?
When is the first bus?	첫 버스는 언제인가요? cheot beo-seu-neun eon-je-in-ga-yo?

When is the last bus?

마지막 버스는
언제인가요?
ma-ji-mak beo-seu-neun
eon-je-in-ga-yo?

stop

정류장
jeong-nyu-jang

next stop

다음 정류장
da-eum jeong-nyu-jang

last stop (terminus)

종점
jong-jeom

Stop here, please.

여기에 세워 주세요.
yeo-gi-e se-wo ju-se-yo.

Excuse me, this is my stop.

실례합니다, 저 여기서
내려요.
sil-lye-ham-ni-da, jeo yeo-gi-seo
nae-ryeo-yo.

Train

train	기차 gi-cha
suburban train	교외 전차 gyo-oe jeon-cha
long-distance train	장거리 기차 jang-geo-ri gi-cha
train station	기차역 gi-cha-yeok
Excuse me, where is the exit to the platform?	실례합니다, 플랫폼으로 가는 출구가 어디인가요? sil-lye-ham-ni-da, peul-laet-po-meu-ro ga-neun chul-gu-ga eo-di-in-ga-yo?

Does this train go to …?	이 기차 …에 가요? i gi-cha ...e ga-yo?
next train	다음 기차 da-eum gi-cha
When is the next train?	다음 기차는 언제인가요? da-eum gi-cha-neun eon-je-in-ga-yo?
Where can I see the schedule?	시간표는 어디서 볼 수 있어요? si-gan-pyo-neun eo-di-seo bol su i-seo-yo?
From which platform?	어느 플랫폼에서 출발해요? eo-neu peul-laet-pom-e-seo chul-bal-hae-yo?
When does the train arrive in …?	기차가 …에 언제 도착해요? gi-cha-ga ...e eon-je do-chak-ae-yo?

Please help me.	도와주세요. do-wa-ju-se-yo.
I'm looking for my seat.	제 좌석을 찾고 있어요. je jwa-seo-geul chat-go i-seo-yo.
We're looking for our seats.	우리 좌석을 찾고 있어요. u-ri jwa-seo-geul chat-go i-seo-yo.

My seat is taken.	제 좌석에 다른 사람이 있어요. je jwa-seo-ge da-reun sa-ram-i i-seo-yo.
Our seats are taken.	우리 좌석에 다른 사람이 있어요. u-ri jwa-seo-ge da-reun sa-ram-i i-seo-yo.

I'm sorry but this is my seat.

죄송하지만 여긴 제
좌석이에요.
joe-song-ha-ji-man nyeo-gin je
jwa-seo-gi-ye-yo.

Is this seat taken?

이 좌석 비었나요?
i jwa-seok bi-eon-na-yo?

May I sit here?

여기 앉아도 되나요?
yeo-gi an-ja-do doe-na-yo?

On the train. Dialogue (No ticket)

Ticket, please.	표 보여주세요. pyo bo-yeo-ju-se-yo.
I don't have a ticket.	표가 없어요. pyo-ga eop-seo-yo.
I lost my ticket.	표를 잃어버렸어요. pyo-reul ri-reo-beo-ryeo-seo-yo.
I forgot my ticket at home.	표를 집에 두고 왔어요. pyo-reul ji-be du-go wa-seo-yo.

You can buy a ticket from me.	저한테 표를 사실 수 있어요. jeo-han-te pyo-reul sa-sil su i-seo-yo.
You will also have to pay a fine.	벌금도 내셔야 해요. beol-geum-do nae-syeo-ya hae-yo.
Okay.	알았어요. a-ra-seo-yo.
Where are you going?	어디까지 가세요? eo-di-kka-ji ga-se-yo?
I'm going to ...	…에 가고 있어요. ... e ga-go i-seo-yo.

How much? I don't understand.	얼마예요? 못 알아들었어요. eol-ma-ye-yo? mot a-ra-deu-reo-seo-yo.
Write it down, please.	적어 주세요. jeo-geo ju-se-yo.
Okay. Can I pay with a credit card?	알았어요. 신용카드 돼요? a-ra-seo-yo. si-nyong-ka-deu dwae-yo?
Yes, you can.	네, 돼요. ne, dwae-yo.

Here's your receipt.	영수증 여기 있어요. yeong-su-jeung yeo-gi i-seo-yo.
Sorry about the fine.	벌금을 내게 되어서 유감이예요. beol-geu-meul lae-ge doe-eo-seo yu-gam-i-ye-yo.
That's okay. It was my fault.	괜찮아요. 제 잘못이예요. gwaen-cha-na-yo. je jal-mo-si-ye-yo.
Enjoy your trip.	즐거운 여행 되세요. jeul-geo-un nyeo-haeng doe-se-yo.

Taxi

taxi	택시 taek-si
taxi driver	택시 운전사 taek-si un-jeon-sa
to catch a taxi	택시를 잡다 taek-si-reul jap-da
taxi stand	택시 정류장 taek-si jeong-nyu-jang
Where can I get a taxi?	어디서 택시를 탈 수 있어요? eo-di-seo taek-si-reul tal su i-seo-yo?
to call a taxi	택시를 부르다. taek-si-reul bu-reu-da.
I need a taxi.	택시가 필요해요. taek-si-ga pi-ryo-hae-yo.
Right now.	지금 당장. ji-geum dang-jang.
What is your address (location)?	주소가 어디예요? ju-so-ga eo-di-ye-yo?
My address is …	제 주소는 …예요. je ju-so-neun …ye-yo.
Your destination?	목적지가 어디예요? mok-jeok-ji-ga eo-di-ye-yo?
Excuse me, …	실례합니다, … sil-lye-ham-ni-da, …
Are you available?	타도 돼요? ta-do dwae-yo?
How much is it to get to …?	…까지 얼마예요? …kka-ji eol-ma-ye-yo?
Do you know where it is?	여기가 어딘지 아세요? yeo-gi-ga eo-din-ji a-se-yo?
Airport, please.	공항까지 가 주세요. gong-hang-kka-ji ga ju-se-yo.
Stop here, please.	여기에 세워 주세요. yeo-gi-e se-wo ju-se-yo.
It's not here.	여기가 아니예요. yeo-gi-ga a-ni-ye-yo.
This is the wrong address.	잘못된 주소예요. jal-mot-doen ju-so-ye-yo.
Turn left.	왼쪽으로 가세요. oen-jjo-geu-ro ga-se-yo.

Turn right.	오른쪽으로 가세요.
	o-reun-jjo-geu-ro ga-se-yo.
How much do I owe you?	얼마 내야 해요?
	eol-ma nae-ya hae-yo?
I'd like a receipt, please.	영수증 주세요.
	yeong-su-jeung ju-se-yo.
Keep the change.	잔돈은 가지세요.
	jan-do-neun ga-ji-se-yo.

Would you please wait for me?	기다려 주시겠어요?
	gi-da-ryeo ju-si-ge-seo-yo?
five minutes	오분
	o-bun
ten minutes	십분
	sip-bun
fifteen minutes	십오 분
	si-bo bun
twenty minutes	이십분
	i-sip-bun
half an hour	삼십분
	sam-sip bun

Hotel

Hello.	안녕하세요. an-nyeong-ha-se-yo.
My name is ...	제 이름은 ··· 입니다. je i-reu-meun ... im-ni-da.
I have a reservation.	예약했어요. ye-yak-ae-seo-yo.
I need ...	··· 필요해요. ... pi-ryo-hae-yo.
a single room	싱글 룸 하나 sing-geul lum ha-na
a double room	더블 룸 하나 deo-beul lum ha-na
How much is that?	저건 얼마예요? jeo-geon eol-ma-ye-yo?
That's a bit expensive.	그건 조금 비싸요. geu-geon jo-geum bi-ssa-yo.
Do you have anything else?	다른 옵션 있어요? da-reun op-syeon i-seo-yo?
I'll take it.	그걸로 할게요. geu-geol-lo hal-ge-yo.
I'll pay in cash.	현금으로 낼게요. hyeon-geu-meu-ro nael-ge-yo.
I've got a problem.	문제가 있어요. mun-je-ga i-seo-yo
My ... is broken.	제 ··· 망가졌어요. je ... mang-ga-jyeo-seo-yo.
My ... is out of order.	제 ··· 고장났어요. je ... go-jang-na-seo-yo.
TV	텔레비전 tel-le-bi-jeon
air conditioner	에어컨 e-eo-keon
tap	수도꼭지 su-do-kkok-ji
shower	샤워기 sya-wo-gi
sink	세면대 se-myeon-dae
safe	금고 geum-go

door lock	도어락 do-eo-rak
electrical outlet	콘센트 kon-sen-teu
hairdryer	헤어 드라이어 he-eo deu-ra-i-eo

I don't have ...	··· 안 나와요. ... an na-wa-yo.
water	물 mul
light	전등 jeon-deung
electricity	전기 jeon-gi

Can you give me ...?	··· 주실 수 있어요? ... ju-sil su i-seo-yo?
a towel	수건 su-geon
a blanket	담요 da-myo
slippers	슬리퍼 seul-li-peo
a robe	가운 ga-un
shampoo	샴푸 syam-pu
soap	비누 bi-nu

I'd like to change rooms.	방을 바꾸고 싶어요. bang-eul ba-kku-go si-peo-yo.
I can't find my key.	열쇠를 못 찾겠어요. yeol-soe-reul mot chat-ge-seo-yo.
Could you open my room, please?	제 방 문을 열어주실 수 있어요? je bang mu-neul ryeo-reo-ju-sil su i-seo-yo?

Who's there?	누구세요? nu-gu-se-yo?
Come in!	들어오세요! deu-reo-o-se-yo!
Just a minute!	잠깐만요! jam-kkan-ma-nyo!

Not right now, please.	지금 당장은 안돼요. ji-geum dang-jang-eun an-dwae-yo.
Come to my room, please.	제 방으로 와 주세요. je bang-eu-ro wa ju-se-yo.

I'd like to order food service.

룸서비스를 받고 싶어요.
rum-seo-bi-seu-reul bat-go si-peo-yo.

My room number is ...

제 방 번호는 ⋯예요.
je bang beon-ho-neun ...ye-yo.

I'm leaving ...

저는 ⋯에 떠나요.
jeo-neun ... e tteo-na-yo.

We're leaving ...

우리는 ⋯에 떠나요.
u-ri-neun ...e tteo-na-yo.

right now

지금 당장
ji-geum dang-jang

this afternoon

오늘 오후
o-neul ro-hu

tonight

오늘밤
o-neul-bam

tomorrow

내일
nae-il

tomorrow morning

내일 아침
nae-il ra-chim

tomorrow evening

내일 저녁
nae-il jeo-nyeok

the day after tomorrow

모레
mo-re

I'd like to pay.

계산하고 싶어요.
gye-san-ha-go si-peo-yo.

Everything was wonderful.

전부 다 아주 좋았어요.
jeon-bu da a-ju jo-a-seo-yo.

Where can I get a taxi?

어디서 택시를 탈 수 있어요?
eo-di-seo taek-si-reul tal su i-seo-yo?

Would you call a taxi for me, please?

택시 불러주실 수 있어요?
taek-si bul-leo-ju-sil su i-seo-yo?

Restaurant

Can I look at the menu, please?	메뉴판 볼 수 있어요? me-nyu-pan bol su i-seo-yo?
Table for one.	한 명이요. han myeong-i-yo.
There are two (three, four) of us.	두 (세, 네) 명이요. du (se, ne) myeong-i-yo.

Smoking	흡연 heu-byeon
No smoking	금연 geu-myeon
Excuse me! (addressing a waiter)	저기요! jeo-gi-yo!
menu	메뉴판 me-nyu-pan
wine list	와인 리스트 wa-in li-seu-teu
The menu, please.	메뉴판 주세요. me-nyu-pan ju-se-yo.

Are you ready to order?	주문하시겠어요? ju-mun-ha-si-ge-seo-yo?
What will you have?	어떤 걸로 하시겠어요? eo-tteon geol-lo ha-si-ge-seo-yo?
I'll have ...	저는 … 할게요. jeo-neun ... hal-ge-yo.

I'm a vegetarian.	저는 채식주의자예요. jeo-neun chae-sik-ju-ui-ja-ye-yo.
meat	고기 go-gi
fish	생선 saeng-seon
vegetables	채소 chae-so

Do you have vegetarian dishes?	채식 메뉴 있어요? chae-sik me-nyu i-seo-yo?
I don't eat pork.	돼지고기 못 먹어요. dwae-ji-go-gi mot meo-geo-yo.
He /she/ doesn't eat meat.	그는 /그녀는/ 고기 못 드세요. geu-neun /geu-nyeo-neun/ go-gi mot deu-se-yo.

I am allergic to ...	저 …에 알러지 있어요. jeo ...e al-leo-ji i-seo-yo.
Would you please bring me ...	… 가져다 주시겠어요? ... ga-jyeo-da ju-si-ge-seo-yo?
salt | pepper | sugar	소금 | 후추 | 설탕 so-geum | hu-chu | seol-tang
coffee | tea | dessert	커피 | 차 | 디저트 keo-pi | cha | di-jeo-teu
water | sparkling | plain	물 | 탄산수 | 생수 mul | tan-san-su | saeng-su
a spoon | fork | knife	숟가락 | 포크 | 나이프 sut-ga-rak | po-keu | na-i-peu
a plate | napkin	앞접시 | 휴지 ap-jeop-si | hyu-ji

Enjoy your meal!	맛있게 드세요! man-nit-ge deu-se-yo!
One more, please.	하나 더 주세요. ha-na deo ju-se-yo.
It was very delicious.	아주 맛있었어요. a-ju man-ni-seo-seo-yo.

check | change | tip	계산서 | 거스름돈 | 팁 gye-san-seo | geo-seu-reum-don | tip
Check, please. (Could I have the check, please?)	계산서 주세요. gye-san-seo ju-se-yo.
Can I pay by credit card?	신용카드 돼요? si-nyong-ka-deu dwae-yo?
I'm sorry, there's a mistake here.	죄송한데 여기 잘못됐어요. joe-song-han-de yeo-gi jal-mot-dwae-seo-yo.

Shopping

Can I help you?	도와드릴까요? do-wa-deu-ril-kka-yo?
Do you have …?	… 있으세요? … i-seu-se-yo?
I'm looking for …	… 찾고 있어요. … chat-go i-seo-yo.
I need …	… 필요해요. … pi-ryo-hae-yo.

I'm just looking.	그냥 구경중이예요. geu-nyang gu-gyeong-jung-i-ye-yo.
We're just looking.	우리 그냥 구경중이예요. u-ri geu-nyang gu-gyeong-jung-i-ye-yo.
I'll come back later.	나중에 다시 올게요. na-jung-e da-si ol-ge-yo.
We'll come back later.	우리 나중에 다시 올게요. u-ri na-jung-e da-si ol-ge-yo.
discounts	sale	할인	세일 ha-rin	se-il

Would you please show me …	… 보여주세요. … bo-yeo-ju-se-yo.
Would you please give me …	… 주세요. … ju-se-yo.
Can I try it on?	입어봐도 돼요? i-beo-bwa-do dwae-yo?
Excuse me, where's the fitting room?	실례합니다, 피팅 룸 어디 있어요? sil-lye-ham-ni-da, pi-ting num eo-di i-seo-yo?
Which color would you like?	다른 색도 있어요? da-reun saek-do i-seo-yo?
size	length	사이즈	길이 sa-i-jeu	gi-ri
How does it fit?	이거 저한테 맞아요? i-geo jeo-han-te ma-ja-yo?

How much is it?	얼마예요? eol-ma-ye-yo?
That's too expensive.	너무 비싸요. neo-mu bi-ssa-yo.
I'll take it.	그걸로 할게요. geu-geol-lo hal-ge-yo.

Excuse me, where do I pay?

실례합니다, 계산 어디서
해요?
sil-lye-ham-ni-da, gye-san eo-di-seo
hae-yo?

Will you pay in cash or credit card?

현금으로 하시겠어요
카드로 하시겠어요?
hyeon-geu-meu-ro ha-si-ge-seo-yo
ka-deu-ro ha-si-ge-seo-yo?

In cash | with credit card

현금으로요 | 카드로요
hyeon-geu-meu-ro-yo | ka-deu-ro-yo

Do you want the receipt?

영수증 드릴까요?
yeong-su-jeung deu-ril-kka-yo?

Yes, please.

네, 주세요.
ne, ju-se-yo.

No, it's OK.

아니오, 괜찮아요.
a-ni-o, gwaen-cha-na-yo.

Thank you. Have a nice day!

감사합니다. 즐거운 하루
되세요!
gam-sa-ham-ni-da. jeul-geo-un ha-ru
doe-se-yo!

In town

Excuse me, please.	실례합니다, 저기요. sil-lye-ham-ni-da, jeo-gi-yo.
I'm looking for …	… 찾고 있어요. … chat-go i-seo-yo.
the subway	지하철 ji-ha-cheol
my hotel	제 호텔 je ho-tel
the movie theater	영화관 yeong-hwa-gwan
a taxi stand	택시 정류장 taek-si jeong-nyu-jang
an ATM	현금인출기 hyeon-geum-in-chul-gi
a foreign exchange office	환전소 hwan-jeon-so
an internet café	피씨방 pi-ssi-bang
… street	…로 …ro
this place	여기 yeo-gi
Do you know where … is?	… 어디인지 아세요? ... eo-di-in-ji a-se-yo?
Which street is this?	여기가 어디예요? yeo-gi-ga eo-di-ye-yo?
Show me where we are right now.	지금 우리가 있는 곳을 보여주세요. ji-geum u-ri-ga in-neun gos-eul bo-yeo-ju-se-yo.
Can I get there on foot?	걸어갈 수 있어요? geo-reo-gal su i-seo-yo?
Do you have a map of the city?	시내 지도 있어요? si-nae ji-do i-seo-yo?
How much is a ticket to get in?	입장권 얼마예요? ip-jang-gwon eol-ma-ye-yo?
Can I take pictures here?	사진 찍어도 돼요? sa-jin jji-geo-do dwae-yo?
Are you open?	열었어요? yeo-reo-seo-yo?

When do you open?

언제 열어요?
eon-je yeo-reo-yo?

When do you close?

언제 닫아요?
eon-je da-da-yo?

Money

money	돈 don
cash	현금 hyeon-geum
paper money	지폐 ji-pye
loose change	동전 dong-jeon
check | change | tip	계산서 | 거스름돈 | 팁 gye-san-seo | geo-seu-reum-don | tip

credit card	카드 ka-deu
wallet	지갑 ji-gap
to buy	사다 sa-da
to pay	내다 nae-da
fine	벌금 beol-geum
free	무료 mu-ryo

Where can I buy ...?	… 어디서 살 수 있어요? … eo-di-seo sal su i-seo-yo?
Is the bank open now?	은행 지금 열었어요? eun-haeng ji-geum myeo-reo-seo-yo?
When does it open?	언제 열어요? eon-je yeo-reo-yo?
When does it close?	언제 닫아요? eon-je da-da-yo?

How much?	얼마예요? eol-ma-ye-yo?
How much is this?	이건 얼마예요? i-geon eol-ma-ye-yo?

That's too expensive.	너무 비싸요. neo-mu bi-ssa-yo.
Excuse me, where do I pay?	실례합니다, 계산 어디서 해요? sil-lye-ham-ni-da, gye-san eo-di-seo hae-yo?

Check, please.

계산서 주세요.
gye-san-seo ju-se-yo.

Can I pay by credit card?

신용카드 돼요?
si-nyong-ka-deu dwae-yo?

Is there an ATM here?

여기 현금인출기 있어요?
yeo-gi hyeon-geum-in-chul-gi i-seo-yo?

I'm looking for an ATM.

현금 인출기를 찾고
있어요.
hyeon-geum in-chul-gi-reul chat-go
i-seo-yo.

I'm looking for a foreign exchange office.

환전소 찾고 있어요.
hwan-jeon-so chat-go i-seo-yo.

I'd like to change ...

··· 환전하고 싶어요.
... hwan-jeon-ha-go si-peo-yo.

What is the exchange rate?

환율 얼마예요?
hwa-nyul reol-ma-ye-yo?

Do you need my passport?

여권 필요해요?
yeo-gwon pi-ryo-hae-yo?

Time

What time is it?	지금 몇 시예요? ji-geum myeot si-ye-yo?
When?	언제요? eon-je-yo?
At what time?	몇 시에요? myeot si-e-yo?
now | later | after ...	지금 | 나중에 | … 이후에 ji-geum | na-jung-e | ... i-hu-e
one o'clock	한 시 han si
one fifteen	한 시 십오 분 han si si-bo bun
one thirty	한 시 삼십 분 han si sam-sip bun
one forty-five	한 시 사십오 분 han si sa-si-bo bun

one | two | three	한 | 두 | 세 han | du | se
four | five | six	네 | 다섯 | 여섯 ne | da-seot | yeo-seot
seven | eight | nine	일곱 | 여덟 | 아홉 il-gop | yeo-deol | a-hop
ten | eleven | twelve	열 | 열한 | 열두 yeol | yeol-han | yeol-du

in ...	… 안에 … an-e
five minutes	오분 o-bun
ten minutes	십분 sip-bun
fifteen minutes	십오분 si-bo bun
twenty minutes	이십분 i-sip-bun
half an hour	삼십분 sam-sip bun
an hour	한 시간 han si-gan
in the morning	아침에 a-chim-e
early in the morning	아침 일쩍 a-chim il-jjik

this morning	오늘 아침 o-neul ra-chim
tomorrow morning	내일 아침 nae-il ra-chim

in the middle of the day	한낮에 han-na-je
in the afternoon	오후에 o-hu-e
in the evening	저녁에 jeo-nyeo-ge
tonight	오늘밤 o-neul-bam

at night	밤에 bam-e
yesterday	어제 eo-je
today	오늘 o-neul
tomorrow	내일 nae-il
the day after tomorrow	모레 mo-re

What day is it today?	오늘이 무슨 요일이예요? o-neu-ri mu-seun nyo-i-ri-ye-yo?
It's ...	… 예요. … ye-yo.
Monday	월요일 wo-ryo-il
Tuesday	화요일 hwa-yo-il
Wednesday	수요일 su-yo-il

Thursday	목요일 mo-gyo-il
Friday	금요일 geu-myo-il
Saturday	토요일 to-yo-il
Sunday	일요일 i-ryo-il

Greetings. Introductions

Hello.	안녕하세요. an-nyeong-ha-se-yo.
Pleased to meet you.	만나서 기쁩니다. man-na-seo gi-ppeum-ni-da.
Me too.	저도요. jeo-do-yo.
I'd like you to meet ...	··· 소개합니다. ... so-gae-ham-ni-da.
Nice to meet you.	만나서 반갑습니다. man-na-seo ban-gap-seum-ni-da.

How are you?	잘 지내셨어요? jal ji-nae-syeo-seo-yo?
My name is ...	제 이름은 ··· 입니다. je i-reu-meun ... im-ni-da.
His name is ...	그의 이름은 ··· 예요. geu-ui i-reu-meun ... ye-yo.
Her name is ...	그녀의 이름은 ··· 예요. geu-nyeo-ui i-reu-meun ... ye-yo.

What's your name?	성함이 어떻게 되세요? seong-ham-i eo-tteo-ke doe-se-yo?
What's his name?	그분 성함이 뭐예요? geu-bun seong-ham-i mwo-ye-yo?
What's her name?	그분 성함이 뭐예요? geu-bun seong-ham-i mwo-ye-yo?

What's your last name?	성이 어떻게 되세요? seong-i eo-tteo-ke doe-se-yo?
You can call me ...	··· 라고 불러 주세요. ... ra-go bul-leo ju-se-yo.
Where are you from?	어디서 오셨어요? eo-di-seo o-syeo-seo-yo?
I'm from ...	··· 에서 왔어요. ... e-seo wa-seo-yo.
What do you do for a living?	무슨 일 하세요? mu-seun il ha-se-yo?

Who is this?	이 분은 누구세요? i bu-neun nu-gu-se-yo?
Who is he?	그 분은 누구세요? geu bu-neun nu-gu-se-yo?
Who is she?	그 분은 누구세요? geu bu-neun nu-gu-se-yo?

Who are they?
그 분들은 누구세요?
geu bun-deu-reun nu-gu-se-yo?

This is ...
이 쪽은 ··· 예요.
i jjo-geun ... ye-yo.

my friend (masc.)
제 친구
je chin-gu

my friend (fem.)
제 친구
je chin-gu

my husband
제 남편
je nam-pyeon

my wife
제 아내
je a-nae

my father
제 아버지
je a-beo-ji

my mother
제 어머니
je eo-meo-ni

my son
제 아들
je a-deul

my daughter
제 딸
je ttal

This is our son.
이 쪽은 우리 아들이예요.
i jjo-geun u-ri a-deu-ri-ye-yo.

This is our daughter.
이 쪽은 우리 딸이예요.
i jjo-geun u-ri tta-ri-ye-yo.

These are my children.
이 쪽은 제 아이들이예요.
i jjo-geun je a-i-deu-ri-ye-yo.

These are our children.
이 쪽은 우리 아이들이예요.
i jjo-geun u-ri a-i-deu-ri-ye-yo.

Farewells

Good bye!	안녕히 계세요! an-nyeong-hi gye-se-yo!
Bye! (inform.)	안녕! an-nyeong!
See you tomorrow.	내일 만나요. nae-il man-na-yo.
See you soon.	곧 만나요. got man-na-yo.
See you at seven.	일곱 시에 만나요. il-gop si-e man-na-yo.
Have fun!	재밌게 놀아! jae-mit-ge no-ra!
Talk to you later.	나중에 봐. na-jung-e bwa.
Have a nice weekend.	주말 잘 보내. ju-mal jal bo-nae.
Good night.	안녕히 주무세요. an-nyeong-hi ju-mu-se-yo.
It's time for me to go.	갈 시간이예요. gal si-gan-i-ye-yo.
I have to go.	가야 해요. ga-ya hae-yo.
I will be right back.	금방 다시 올게요. geum-bang da-si ol-ge-yo.
It's late.	늦었어요. neu-jeo-seo-yo.
I have to get up early.	일찍 일어나야 해요. il-jjik gi-reo-na-ya hae-yo.
I'm leaving tomorrow.	내일 떠나요. nae-il tteo-na-yo.
We're leaving tomorrow.	우리는 내일 떠나요. u-ri-neun nae-il tteo-na-yo.
Have a nice trip!	즐거운 여행 되세요! jeul-geo-un nyeo-haeng doe-se-yo!
It was nice meeting you.	만나서 반가웠어요. man-na-seo ban-ga-wo-seo-yo.
It was nice talking to you.	이야기하느라 즐거웠어요. i-ya-gi-ha-neu-ra jeul-geo-wo-seo-yo.
Thanks for everything.	전부 다 감사합니다. jeon-bu da gam-sa-ham-ni-da.

I had a very good time.

아주 즐거웠어요.
a-ju jeul-geo-wo-seo-yo.

We had a very good time.

우리는 아주 즐거웠어요.
u-ri-neun a-ju jeul-geo-wo-seo-yo.

It was really great.

정말 멋졌어요.
jeong-mal meot-jyeo-seo-yo.

I'm going to miss you.

보고 싶을 거예요.
bo-go si-peul geo-ye-yo.

We're going to miss you.

우리는 당신이 보고 싶을
거예요.
u-ri-neun dang-sin-i bo-go si-peul
geo-ye-yo.

Good luck!

행운을 빌어!
haeng-u-neul bi-reo!

Say hi to …

… 에게 안부 전해 주세요.
… e-ge an-bu jeon-hae ju-se-yo.

Foreign language

I don't understand.	못 알아들었어요. mot a-ra-deu-reo-seo-yo.
Write it down, please.	적어 주세요. jeo-geo ju-se-yo.
Do you speak …?	… 하실 수 있어요? … ha-sil su i-seo-yo?
I speak a little bit of …	저는 … 조금 할 수 있어요. jeo-neun … jo-geum hal su i-seo-yo.
English	영어 yeong-eo
Turkish	터키어 teo-ki-eo
Arabic	아랍어 a-ra-beo
French	프랑스어 peu-rang-seu-eo
German	독일어 do-gi-reo
Italian	이탈리아어 i-tal-li-a-eo
Spanish	스페인어 seu-pe-in-eo
Portuguese	포르투갈어 po-reu-tu-ga-reo
Chinese	중국어 jung-gu-geo
Japanese	일본어 il-bon-eo
Can you repeat that, please.	다시 한 번 말해 주세요. da-si han beon mal-hae ju-se-yo.
I understand.	알아들었어요. a-ra-deu-reo-seo-yo.
I don't understand.	못 알아들었어요. mot a-ra-deu-reo-seo-yo.
Please speak more slowly.	좀 더 천천히 말해 주세요. jom deo cheon-cheon-hi mal-hae ju-se-yo.

Is that correct? (Am I saying it right?)   이거 맞아요?
i-geo ma-ja-yo?

What is this? (What does this mean?)   이게 뭐예요?
i-ge mwo-ye-yo?

Apologies

Excuse me, please.
실례합니다, 저기요.
sil-lye-ham-ni-da, jeo-gi-yo.

I'm sorry.
죄송합니다.
joe-song-ham-ni-da.

I'm really sorry.
정말 죄송합니다.
jeong-mal joe-song-ham-ni-da.

Sorry, it's my fault.
죄송해요, 제 잘못이예요.
joe-song-hae-yo, je jal-mo-si-ye-yo.

My mistake.
제 실수예요.
je sil-su-ye-yo.

May I ...?
…해도 되나요?
... hae-do doe-na-yo?

Do you mind if I ...?
…해도 괜찮으세요?
...hae-do gwaen-cha-neu-se-yo?

It's OK.
괜찮아요.
gwaen-cha-na-yo.

It's all right.
괜찮아요.
gwaen-cha-na-yo.

Don't worry about it.
걱정하지 마세요.
geok-jeong-ha-ji ma-se-yo.

Agreement

Yes.	네. ne.
Yes, sure.	네, 물론입니다. ne, mul-lon-im-ni-da.
OK (Good!)	좋아요. jo-a-yo.
Very well.	아주 좋아요. a-ju jo-a-yo.
Certainly!	당연합니다! dang-yeon-ham-ni-da!
I agree.	동의해요. dong-ui-hae-yo.
That's correct.	정확해요. jeong-hwak-ae-yo.
That's right.	그게 맞아요. geu-ge ma-ja-yo.
You're right.	당신이 맞아요. dang-sin-i ma-ja-yo.
I don't mind.	저는 신경 쓰지 않아요. jeo-neun sin-gyeong sseu-ji a-na-yo.
Absolutely right.	확실히 맞아요. hwak-sil-hi ma-ja-yo.
It's possible.	가능해요. ga-neung-hae-yo.
That's a good idea.	좋은 생각이예요. jo-eun saeng-ga-gi-ye-yo.
I can't say no.	아니라고 할 수 없어요. a-ni-ra-go hal su eop-seo-yo.
I'd be happy to.	기쁘게 할게요. gi-ppeu-ge hal-ge-yo.
With pleasure.	기꺼이요. gi-kkeo-i-yo.

Refusal. Expressing doubt

No.
아니오.
a-ni-o.

Certainly not.
절대 아니예요.
jeol-dae a-ni-ye-yo.

I don't agree.
동의할 수 없어요.
dong-ui-hal su eop-seo-yo.

I don't think so.
그렇게 생각 안 해요.
geu-reo-ke saeng-gak gan hae-yo.

It's not true.
그렇지 않아요.
geu-reo-chi a-na-yo.

You are wrong.
틀렸어요.
teul-lyeo-seo-yo.

I think you are wrong.
틀리신 거 같아요.
teul-li-sin geo ga-ta-yo.

I'm not sure.
잘 모르겠어요.
jal mo-reu-ge-seo-yo.

It's impossible.
불가능해요.
bul-ga-neung-hae-yo.

Nothing of the kind (sort)!
그럴 리가요!
geu-reol li-ga-yo!

The exact opposite.
정 반대예요.
jeong ban-dae-ye-yo.

I'm against it.
저는 반대예요.
jeo-neun ban-dae-ye-yo.

I don't care.
저는 신경 안 써요.
jeo-neun sin-gyeong an sseo-yo.

I have no idea.
모르겠어요.
mo-reu-ge-seo-yo.

I doubt it.
그건 아닌 것 같아요.
geu-geon a-nin geot ga-ta-yo.

Sorry, I can't.
죄송합니다. 못 해요.
joe-song-ham-ni-da. mot tae-yo.

Sorry, I don't want to.
죄송합니다. 하기 싫어요.
joe-song-ham-ni-da. ha-gi si-reo-yo.

Thank you, but I don't need this.
감사합니다, 하지만 필요 없어요.
gam-sa-ham-ni-da, ha-ji-man pi-ryo eop-seo-yo.

It's getting late.
좀 늦었네요.
jom neu-jeon-ne-yo.

I have to get up early.

일찍 일어나야 해요.
il-jjik gi-reo-na-ya hae-yo.

I don't feel well.

몸이 안 좋아요.
mom-i an jo-a-yo.

Expressing gratitude

Thank you.
감사합니다.
gam-sa-ham-ni-da.

Thank you very much.
대단히 감사합니다.
dae-dan-hi gam-sa-ham-ni-da.

I really appreciate it.
정말로 감사히
생각해요.
jeong-mal-lo gam-sa-hi
saeng-gak-ae-yo.

I'm really grateful to you.
당신에게 정말로
감사해요.
dang-sin-e-ge jeong-mal-lo
gam-sa-hae-yo.

We are really grateful to you.
저희는 당신에게 정말로
감사해요.
jeo-hui-neun dang-sin-e-ge jeong-mal-lo
gam-sa-hae-yo.

Thank you for your time.
시간 내 주셔서
감사합니다.
si-gan nae ju-syeo-seo
gam-sa-ham-ni-da.

Thanks for everything.
전부 다 감사합니다.
jeon-bu da gam-sa-ham-ni-da.

Thank you for ...
…에 대해 감사합니다.
...e dae-hae gam-sa-ham-ni-da.

your help
도움
do-um

a nice time
즐거운 시간
jeul-geo-un si-gan

a wonderful meal
훌륭한 식사
hul-lyung-han sik-sa

a pleasant evening
만족스러운 저녁
man-jok-seu-reo-un jeo-nyeok

a wonderful day
훌륭한 하루
hul-lyung-han ha-ru

an amazing journey
근사한 여행
geun-sa-han nyeo-haeng

Don't mention it.
별 말씀을요.
byeol mal-sseu-meu-ryo.

You are welcome.
천만에요.
cheon-man-e-yo.

Any time.
언제든지요.
eon-je-deun-ji-yo.

My pleasure.

제가 즐거웠어요.
je-ga jeul-geo-wo-seo-yo.

Forget it.

됐어요.
dwae-seo-yo.

Don't worry about it.

걱정하지 마세요.
geok-jeong-ha-ji ma-se-yo.

Congratulations. Best wishes

Congratulations!	축하합니다! chuk-a-ham-ni-da!
Happy birthday!	생일 축하합니다! saeng-il chuk-a-ham-ni-da!
Merry Christmas!	메리 크리스마스! me-ri keu-ri-seu-ma-seu!
Happy New Year!	새해 복 많이 받으세요! sae-hae bok ma-ni ba-deu-se-yo!

Happy Easter!	즐거운 부활절 되세요! jeul-geo-un bu-hwal-jeol doe-se-yo!
Happy Hanukkah!	즐거운 하누카 되세요! jeul-geo-un ha-nu-ka doe-se-yo!

I'd like to propose a toast.	건배해요. geon-bae-hae-yo.
Cheers!	건배! geon-bae!
Let's drink to …!	… 위하여! ... wi-ha-yeo!
To our success!	성공을 위하여! seong-gong-eul rwi-ha-yeo!
To your success!	성공을 위하여! seong-gong-eul rwi-ha-yeo!

Good luck!	행운을 빌어! haeng-u-neul bi-reo!
Have a nice day!	좋은 하루 되세요! jo-eun ha-ru doe-se-yo!
Have a good holiday!	좋은 휴일 되세요! jo-eun hyu-il doe-se-yo!
Have a safe journey!	안전한 여행 되세요! an-jeon-han nyeo-haeng doe-se-yo!
I hope you get better soon!	빨리 나으세요! ppal-li na-eu-se-yo!

Socializing

Why are you sad?	왜 슬퍼하세요? wae seul-peo-ha-se-yo?
Smile! Cheer up!	웃으세요! 기운 내세요! us-eu-se-yo! gi-un nae-se-yo!
Are you free tonight?	오늘 밤에 시간 있으세요? o-neul bam-e si-gan i-seu-se-yo?
May I offer you a drink?	제가 한 잔 살까요? je-ga han jan sal-kka-yo?
Would you like to dance?	춤 추실래요? chum chu-sil-lae-yo?
Let's go to the movies.	영화 보러 갑시다. yeong-hwa bo-reo gap-si-da.
May I invite you to …?	…에 초대해도 될까요? ...e cho-dae-hae-do doel-kka-yo?
a restaurant	음식점 eum-sik-jeom
the movies	영화관 yeong-hwa-gwan
the theater	극장 geuk-jang
go for a walk	산책 san-chaek
At what time?	몇 시예요? myeot si-e-yo?
tonight	오늘밤 o-neul-bam
at six	여섯 시 yeo-seot si
at seven	일곱 시 il-gop si
at eight	여덟 시 yeo-deol si
at nine	아홉 시 a-hop si
Do you like it here?	여기가 마음에 드세요? yeo-gi-ga ma-eum-e deu-se-yo?
Are you here with someone?	누구랑 같이 왔어요? nu-gu-rang ga-chi wa-seo-yo?
I'm with my friend.	친구랑 같이 왔어요. chin-gu-rang ga-chi wa-seo-yo.

I'm with my friends.	친구들이랑 같이 왔어요.
	chin-gu-deu-ri-rang ga-chi wa-seo-yo.
No, I'm alone.	아니오, 혼자 왔어요.
	a-ni-o, hon-ja wa-seo-yo.

Do you have a boyfriend?	남자친구 있어?
	nam-ja-chin-gu i-seo?
I have a boyfriend.	남자친구 있어.
	nam-ja-chin-gu i-seo.
Do you have a girlfriend?	여자친구 있어?
	yeo-ja-chin-gu i-seo?
I have a girlfriend.	여자친구 있어.
	yeo-ja-chin-gu i-seo.

Can I see you again?	다시 만날래?
	da-si man-nal-lae?
Can I call you?	전화해도 돼?
	jeon-hwa-hae-do dwae?
Call me. (Give me a call.)	전화해 줘.
	jeon-hwa-hae jwo.
What's your number?	전화번호가 뭐야?
	jeon-hwa-beon-ho-ga mwo-ya?
I miss you.	보고싶어.
	bo-go-si-peo.

You have a beautiful name.	이름이 아름다우시네요.
	i-reum-i a-reum-da-u-si-ne-yo.
I love you.	사랑해.
	sa-rang-hae.
Will you marry me?	결혼해 줄래?
	gyeol-hon-hae jul-lae?
You're kidding!	장난치지 마세요!
	jang-nan-chi-ji ma-se-yo!
I'm just kidding.	장난이었어요.
	jang-nan-i-eo-seo-yo.

Are you serious?	진심이세요?
	jin-sim-i-se-yo?
I'm serious.	진심이예요.
	jin-sim-i-ye-yo.
Really?!	정말로요?!
	jeong-mal-lo-yo?!
It's unbelievable!	믿을 수 없어요!
	mi-deul su eop-seo-yo!
I don't believe you.	당신을 믿지 않아요.
	dang-si-neul mit-ji a-na-yo.

I can't.	그럴 수 없어요.
	geu-reol su eop-seo-yo.
I don't know.	모르겠어요.
	mo-reu-ge-seo-yo.

I don't understand you.	무슨 말인지 모르겠어요. mu-seun ma-rin-ji mo-reu-ge-seo-yo.
Please go away.	저리 가세요. jeo-ri ga-se-yo.
Leave me alone!	혼자 있고 싶어요! hon-ja it-go si-peo-yo!
I can't stand him.	그를 견딜 수 없어요. geu-reul gyeon-dil su eop-seo-yo.
You are disgusting!	당신 역겨워요! dang-sin nyeok-gyeo-wo-yo!
I'll call the police!	경찰을 부를 거예요! gyeong-cha-reul bu-reul geo-ye-yo!

Sharing impressions. Emotions

I like it.	마음에 들어요. ma-eum-e deu-reo-yo.
Very nice.	아주 좋아요. a-ju jo-a-yo.
That's great!	멋져요! meot-jyeo-yo!
It's not bad.	나쁘지 않아요. na-ppeu-ji a-na-yo.

I don't like it.	마음에 들지 않아요. ma-eum-e deul-ji a-na-yo.
It's not good.	좋지 않아요. jo-chi a-na-yo.
It's bad.	나빠요. na-ppa-yo.
It's very bad.	아주 나빠요. a-ju na-ppa-yo.
It's disgusting.	역겨워요. yeok-gyeo-wo-yo.

I'm happy.	저는 행복해요. jeo-neun haeng-bok-ae-yo.
I'm content.	저는 만족해요. jeo-neun man-jok-ae-yo.
I'm in love.	저는 사랑에 빠졌어요. jeo-neun sa-rang-e ppa-jyeo-seo-yo.
I'm calm.	저는 침착해요. jeo-neun chim-chak-ae-yo.
I'm bored.	저는 지루해요. jeo-neun ji-ru-hae-yo.

I'm tired.	저는 지쳤어요. jeo-neun ji-chyeo-seo-yo.
I'm sad.	저는 슬퍼요. jeo-neun seul-peo-yo.
I'm frightened.	저는 무서워요. jeo-neun mu-seo-wo-yo.

I'm angry.	저는 화났어요. jeo-neun hwa-na-seo-yo.
I'm worried.	저는 걱정이 돼요. jeo-neun geok-jeong-i dwae-yo.
I'm nervous.	저는 긴장이 돼요. jeo-neun gin-jang-i dwae-yo.

I'm jealous. (envious)   저는 부러워요.
jeo-neun bu-reo-wo-yo.

I'm surprised.   놀랐어요.
nol-la-seo-yo.

I'm perplexed.   당황했어요.
dang-hwang-hae-seo-yo.

Problems. Accidents

I've got a problem.	문제가 있어요. mun-je-ga i-seo-yo.
We've got a problem.	우리는 문제가 있어요. u-ri-neun mun-je-ga i-seo-yo.
I'm lost.	길을 잃었어요. gi-reul ri-reo-seo-yo.
I missed the last bus (train).	마지막 버스 (기차)를 놓쳤어요. ma-ji-mak beo-seu (gi-cha)reul lo-chyeo-seo-yo.
I don't have any money left.	돈이 다 떨어졌어요. don-i da tteo-reo-jyeo-seo-yo.

I've lost my ...	… 잃어버렸어요. ... i-reo-beo-ryeo-seo-yo.
Someone stole my ...	제 … 누가 훔쳐갔어요. je ... nu-ga hum-chyeo-ga-seo-yo.
passport	여권 yeo-gwon
wallet	지갑 ji-gap
papers	서류 seo-ryu
ticket	표 pyo
money	돈 don
handbag	핸드백 haen-deu-baek
camera	카메라 ka-me-ra
laptop	노트북 no-teu-buk
tablet computer	타블렛피씨 ta-beul-let-pi-ssi
mobile phone	핸드폰 haen-deu-pon

Help me!	도와주세요! do-wa-ju-se-yo!
What's happened?	무슨 일이 있었어요? mu-seun i-ri i-seo-seo-yo?
fire	화재 hwa-jae

shooting	총격 chong-gyeok
murder	살인 sa-rin
explosion	폭발 pok-bal
fight	폭행 pok-aeng

Call the police!	경찰을 불러 주세요! gyeong-cha-reul bul-leo ju-se-yo!
Please hurry up!	제발 서둘러요! je-bal seo-dul-leo-yo!
I'm looking for the police station.	경찰서를 찾고 있어요. gyeong-chal-seo-reul chat-go i-seo-yo.
I need to make a call.	전화를 걸어야 해요. jeon-hwa-reul geo-reo-ya hae-yo.
May I use your phone?	전화를 빌려주실 수 있어요? jeon-hwa-reul bil-lyeo-ju-sil su i-seo-yo?

I've been ...	저는 … 당했어요. jeo-neun ... dang-hae-seo-yo.
mugged	강도 gang-do
robbed	도둑질 do-duk-jil
raped	강간 gang-gan
attacked (beaten up)	폭행 pok-aeng

Are you all right?	괜찮으세요? gwaen-cha-neu-se-yo?
Did you see who it was?	누구였는지 보셨어요? nu-gu-yeon-neun-ji bo-syeo-seo-yo?
Would you be able to recognize the person?	그 사람을 알아볼 수 있겠어요? geu sa-ra-meul ra-ra-bol su it-ge-seo-yo?
Are you sure?	확실해요? hwak-sil-hae-yo?

Please calm down.	제발 진정해요. je-bal jin-jeong-hae-yo.
Take it easy!	마음을 가라앉히세요! ma-eu-meul ga-ra-an-chi-se-yo!
Don't worry!	걱정하지 마세요! geok-jeong-ha-ji ma-se-yo!
Everything will be fine.	다 잘 될 거예요. da jal doel geo-ye-yo.
Everything's all right.	다 괜찮아요. da gwaen-cha-na-yo.

Come here, please.

이 쪽으로 오세요.
i jjo-geu-ro o-se-yo.

I have some questions for you.

질문이 있습니다.
jil-mun-i it-seum-ni-da.

Wait a moment, please.

잠시 기다려 주세요.
jam-si gi-da-ryeo ju-se-yo.

Do you have any I.D.?

신분증 있습니까?
sin-bun-jeung it-seum-ni-kka?

Thanks. You can leave now.

감사합니다. 이제 가셔도
됩니다.
gam-sa-ham-ni-da. i-je ga-syeo-do
doem-ni-da.

Hands behind your head!

손 머리 위로 들어!
son meo-ri wi-ro deu-reo!

You're under arrest!

체포한다!
che-po-han-da!

Health problems

Please help me.	도와주세요. do-wa-ju-se-yo.
I don't feel well.	몸이 안 좋아요. mom-i an jo-a-yo.
My husband doesn't feel well.	제 남편이 몸이 안 좋아요. je nam-pyeon-i mom-i an jo-a-yo.
My son …	제 아들이 … je a-deu-ri …
My father …	제 아버지가 … je a-beo-ji-ga …
My wife doesn't feel well.	제 아내가 몸이 안 좋아요. je a-nae-ga mom-i an jo-a-yo.
My daughter …	제 딸이 … je tta-ri …
My mother …	제 어머니가 … je eo-meo-ni-ga …
I've got a …	…이 있어요. …i i-seo-yo.
headache	두통 du-tong
sore throat	인후통 in-hu-tong
stomach ache	복통 bok-tong
toothache	치통 chi-tong
I feel dizzy.	어지러워요. eo-ji-reo-wo-yo.
He has a fever.	그는 열이 있어요. geu-neun nyeo-ri i-seo-yo.
She has a fever.	그녀는 열이 있어요. geu-nyeo-neun nyeo-ri i-seo-yo.
I can't breathe.	숨을 못 쉬겠어요. su-meul mot swi-ge-seo-yo.
I'm short of breath.	숨이 차요. sum-i cha-yo.
I am asthmatic.	저는 천식이 있어요. jeo-neun cheon-si-gi i-seo-yo.
I am diabetic.	저는 당뇨가 있어요. jeo-neun dang-nyo-ga i-seo-yo.

| I can't sleep. | 저는 잠을 못 자요.
jeo-neun ja-meul mot ja-yo. |
| food poisoning | 식중독
sik-jung-dok |

It hurts here.	여기가 아파요. yeo-gi-ga a-pa-yo.
Help me!	도와주세요! do-wa-ju-se-yo!
I am here!	여기 있어요! yeo-gi i-seo-yo!
We are here!	우리 여기 있어요! u-ri yeo-gi i-seo-yo!
Get me out of here!	꺼내주세요! kkeo-nae-ju-se-yo!
I need a doctor.	의사가 필요해요. ui-sa-ga pi-ryo-hae-yo.
I can't move.	못 움직이겠어요. mot um-ji-gi-ge-seo-yo.
I can't move my legs.	다리를 못 움직이겠어요. da-ri-reul mot um-ji-gi-ge-seo-yo.

I have a wound.	다쳤어요. da-chyeo-seo-yo.
Is it serious?	심각한가요? sim-gak-an-ga-yo?
My documents are in my pocket.	주머니에 제 서류가 있어요. ju-meo-ni-e je seo-ryu-ga i-seo-yo.
Calm down!	진정해요! jin-jeong-hae-yo!
May I use your phone?	전화를 빌려주실 수 있어요? jeon-hwa-reul bil-lyeo-ju-sil su i-seo-yo?

Call an ambulance!	구급차를 불러 주세요! gu-geup-cha-reul bul-leo ju-se-yo!
It's urgent!	급해요! geu-pae-yo!
It's an emergency!	긴급 상황이에요! gin-geup sang-hwang-i-e-yo!
Please hurry up!	제발 서둘러요! je-bal seo-dul-leo-yo!
Would you please call a doctor?	의사를 불러주시겠어요? ui-sa-reul bul-leo-ju-si-ge-seo-yo?
Where is the hospital?	병원은 어디 있어요? byeong-wo-neun eo-di i-seo-yo?

How are you feeling?	기분이 어떠세요? gi-bun-i eo-tteo-se-yo?
Are you all right?	괜찮으세요? gwaen-cha-neu-se-yo?
What's happened?	무슨 일이 있었어요? mu-seun i-ri i-seo-seo-yo?

I feel better now.

이제 나아졌어요.
i-je na-a-jyeo-seo-yo.

It's OK.

괜찮아요.
gwaen-cha-na-yo.

It's all right.

괜찮아요.
gwaen-cha-na-yo.

At the pharmacy

pharmacy (drugstore)	약국 yak-guk
24-hour pharmacy	24시간 약국 i-sip-sa-si-gan nyak-guk
Where is the closest pharmacy?	가장 가까운 약국이 어디예요? ga-jang ga-kka-un nyak-gu-gi eo-di-ye-yo?
Is it open now?	지금 열었어요? ji-geum myeo-reo-seo-yo?
At what time does it open?	몇 시에 열어요? myeot si-e yeo-reo-yo?
At what time does it close?	몇 시에 닫아요? myeot si-e da-da-yo?
Is it far?	멀어요? meo-reo-yo?
Can I get there on foot?	걸어갈 수 있어요? geo-reo-gal su i-seo-yo?
Can you show me on the map?	지도에서 보여주실 수 있어요? ji-do-e-seo bo-yeo-ju-sil su i-seo-yo?
Please give me something for ...	…에 듣는 약 주세요. ...e deun-neun nyak ju-se-yo.
a headache	두통 du-tong
a cough	기침 gi-chim
a cold	감기 gam-gi
the flu	독감 dok-gam
a fever	열 yeol
a stomach ache	복통 bok-tong
nausea	구토 gu-to
diarrhea	설사 seol-sa
constipation	변비 byeon-bi

pain in the back	등 통증 deung tong-jeung
chest pain	가슴 통증 ga-seum tong-jeung
side stitch	옆구리 당김 yeop-gu-ri dang-gim
abdominal pain	배 통증 bae tong-jeung

pill	알약 a-ryak
ointment, cream	연고 yeon-go
syrup	물약 mul-lyak
spray	스프레이 seu-peu-re-i
drops	안약 a-nyak

You need to go to the hospital.	병원에 가셔야 해요. byeong-won-e ga-syeo-ya hae-yo.
health insurance	건강보험 geon-gang-bo-heom
prescription	처방전 cheo-bang-jeon
insect repellant	방충제 bang-chung-je
Band Aid	밴드에이드 baen-deu-e-i-deu

The bare minimum

Excuse me, ...	실례합니다, ··· sil-lye-ham-ni-da, ...
Hello.	안녕하세요. an-nyeong-ha-se-yo.
Thank you.	감사합니다. gam-sa-ham-ni-da.
Good bye.	안녕히 계세요. an-nyeong-hi gye-se-yo.
Yes.	네. ne.
No.	아니오. a-ni-o.
I don't know.	모르겠어요. mo-reu-ge-seo-yo.
Where?	Where to?	When?	어디예요?	어디까지 가세요? | 언제요? eo-di-ye-yo?	eo-di-kka-ji ga-se-yo? | eon-je-yo?

I need ...	··· 필요해요. ... pi-ryo-hae-yo.
I want ...	··· 싶어요. ... si-peo-yo.
Do you have ...?	··· 있으세요? ... i-seu-se-yo?
Is there a ... here?	여기 ··· 있어요? yeo-gi ... i-seo-yo?
May I ...?	···해도 되나요? ... hae-do doe-na-yo?
..., please (polite request)	···, 부탁합니다. ..., bu-tak-am-ni-da.

I'm looking for ...	··· 찾고 있어요. ... chat-go i-seo-yo.
restroom	화장실 hwa-jang-sil
ATM	현금인출기 hyeon-geum-in-chul-gi
pharmacy (drugstore)	약국 yak-guk
hospital	병원 byeong-won
police station	경찰서 gyeong-chal-seo

subway	지하철 ji-ha-cheol
taxi	택시 taek-si
train station	기차역 gi-cha-yeok

My name is ...	제 이름은 … 입니다. je i-reu-meun ... im-ni-da.
What's your name?	성함이 어떻게 되세요? seong-ham-i eo-tteo-ke doe-se-yo?
Could you please help me?	도와주세요. do-wa-ju-se-yo.
I've got a problem.	문제가 있어요. mun-je-ga i-seo-yo.
I don't feel well.	몸이 안 좋아요. mom-i an jo-a-yo.
Call an ambulance!	구급차를 불러 주세요! gu-geup-cha-reul bul-leo ju-se-yo!
May I make a call?	전화를 써도 되나요? jeon-hwa-reul sseo-do doe-na-yo?

I'm sorry.	죄송합니다. joe-song-ham-ni-da.
You're welcome.	천만에요. cheon-man-e-yo.

I, me	저 jeo
you (inform.)	너 neo
he	그 geu
she	그녀 geu-nyeo
they (masc.)	그들 geu-deul
they (fem.)	그들 geu-deul
we	우리 u-ri
you (pl)	너희 neo-hui
you (sg, form.)	당신 dang-sin

ENTRANCE	입구 ip-gu
EXIT	출구 chul-gu
OUT OF ORDER	고장 go-jang

CLOSED
닫힘
da-chim

OPEN
열림
yeol-lim

FOR WOMEN
여성용
yeo-seong-yong

FOR MEN
남성용
nam-seong-yong

TOPICAL
VOCABULARY

This section contains more
than 3,000 of the most
important words.
The dictionary will provide
invaluable assistance while
traveling abroad, because
frequently individual words
are enough for you to be
understood.
The dictionary includes a
convenient transcription of
each foreign word

T&P Books Publishing

VOCABULARY
CONTENTS

T&P Books Publishing

BASIC CONCEPTS

T&P Books Publishing

1. Pronouns

I, me	나, 저	na
you	너	neo
he	그, 그분	geu, geu-bun
she	그녀	geu-nyeo
it	그것	geu-geot
we	우리	u-ri
you (to a group)	너희	neo-hui
you (polite, sing.)	당신	dang-sin
they	그들	geu-deul

2. Greetings. Salutations

Hello! (fam.)	안녕!	an-nyeong!
Hello! (form.)	안녕하세요!	an-nyeong-ha-se-yo!
Good morning!	안녕하세요!	an-nyeong-ha-se-yo!
Good afternoon!	안녕하세요!	an-nyeong-ha-se-yo!
Good evening!	안녕하세요!	an-nyeong-ha-se-yo!
to say hello	인사하다	in-sa-ha-da
Hi! (hello)	안녕!	an-nyeong!
greeting (n)	인사	in-sa
to greet (vt)	인사하다	in-sa-ha-da
How are you?	잘 지내세요?	jal ji-nae-se-yo?
What's new?	어떻게 지내?	eo-tteo-ke ji-nae?
Bye-Bye! Goodbye!	안녕히 가세요!	an-nyeong-hi ga-se-yo!
See you soon!	또 만나요!	tto man-na-yo!
Farewell! (to a friend)	잘 있어!	jal ri-seo!
Farewell! (form.)	안녕히 계세요!	an-nyeong-hi gye-se-yo!
to say goodbye	작별인사를 하다	jak-byeo-rin-sa-reul ha-da
So long!	안녕!	an-nyeong!
Thank you!	감사합니다!	gam-sa-ham-ni-da!
Thank you very much!	대단히 감사합니다!	dae-dan-hi gam-sa-ham-ni-da!
You're welcome	천만이에요	cheon-man-i-e-yo
Don't mention it!	천만의 말씀입니다	cheon-man-ui mal-sseum-im-ni-da
It was nothing	천만에	cheon-man-e
Excuse me! (fam.)	실례!	sil-lye!

Excuse me! (form.)	실례합니다!	sil-lye-ham-ni-da!
to excuse (forgive)	용서하다	yong-seo-ha-da
to apologize (vi)	사과하다	sa-gwa-ha-da
My apologies	사과드립니다	sa-gwa-deu-rim-ni-da
I'm sorry!	죄송합니다!	joe-song-ham-ni-da!
to forgive (vt)	용서하다	yong-seo-ha-da
please (adv)	부탁합니다	bu-tak-am-ni-da
Don't forget!	잊지 마십시오!	it-ji ma-sip-si-o!
Certainly!	물론이에요!	mul-lon-i-e-yo!
Of course not!	물론 아니에요!	mul-lon a-ni-e-yo!
Okay! (I agree)	그래요!	geu-rae-yo!
That's enough!	그만!	geu-man!

3. Questions

Who?	누구?	nu-gu?
What?	무엇?	mu-eot?
Where? (at, in)	어디?	eo-di?
Where (to)?	어디로?	eo-di-ro?
From where?	어디로부터?	eo-di-ro-bu-teo?
When?	언제?	eon-je?
Why? (What for?)	왜?	wae?
Why? (~ are you crying?)	왜?	wae?
What for?	무엇을 위해서?	mu-eos-eul rwi-hae-seo?
How? (in what way)	어떻게?	eo-tteo-ke?
What? (What kind of ...?)	어떤?	eo-tteon?
Which?	어느?	eo-neu?
To whom?	누구에게?	nu-gu-e-ge?
About whom?	누구에 대하여?	nu-gu-e dae-ha-yeo?
About what?	무엇에 대하여?	mu-eos-e dae-ha-yeo?
With whom?	누구하고?	nu-gu-ha-go?
How many? How much?	얼마?	eol-ma?
Whose?	누구의?	nu-gu-ui?

4. Prepositions

with (accompanied by)	··· 하고	... ha-go
without	없이	eop-si
to (indicating direction)	··· 에	... e
about (talking ~ ...)	··· 에 대하여	... e dae-ha-yeo
before (in time)	전에	jeon-e
in front of ...	··· 앞에	... a-pe
under (beneath, below)	밑에	mi-te

above (over)	위에	wi-e
on (atop)	위에	wi-e
from (off, out of)	··· 에서	... e-seo
of (made from)	··· 로	... ro
in (e.g., ~ ten minutes)	··· 안에	... a-ne
over (across the top of)	너머	dwi-e

5. Function words. Adverbs. Part 1

Where? (at, in)	어디?	eo-di?
here (adv)	여기	yeo-gi
there (adv)	거기	geo-gi
somewhere (to be)	어딘가	eo-din-ga
nowhere (not anywhere)	어디도	eo-di-do
by (near, beside)	옆에	yeo-pe
by the window	창문 옆에	chang-mun nyeo-pe
Where (to)?	어디로?	eo-di-ro?
here (e.g., come ~!)	여기로	yeo-gi-ro
there (e.g., to go ~)	거기로	geo-gi-ro
from here (adv)	여기서	yeo-gi-seo
from there (adv)	거기서	geo-gi-seo
close (adv)	가까이	ga-kka-i
far (adv)	멀리	meol-li
near (e.g., ~ Paris)	근처에	geun-cheo-e
nearby (adv)	인근에	in-geu-ne
not far (adv)	멀지 않게	meol-ji an-ke
left (adj)	왼쪽의	oen-jjo-gui
on the left	왼쪽에	oen-jjo-ge
to the left	왼쪽으로	oen-jjo-geu-ro
right (adj)	오른쪽의	o-reun-jjo-gui
on the right	오른쪽에	o-reun-jjo-ge
to the right	오른쪽으로	o-reun-jjo-geu-ro
in front (adv)	앞쪽에	ap-jjo-ge
front (as adj)	앞의	a-pui
ahead (the kids ran ~)	앞으로	a-peu-ro
behind (adv)	뒤에	dwi-e
from behind	뒤에서	dwi-e-seo
back (towards the rear)	뒤로	dwi-ro
middle	가운데	ga-un-de
in the middle	가운데에	ga-un-de-e

at the side	옆에	yeo-pe
everywhere (adv)	모든 곳에	mo-deun gos-e
around (in all directions)	주위에	ju-wi-e
from inside	내면에서	nae-myeon-e-seo
somewhere (to go)	어딘가에	eo-din-ga-e
straight (directly)	똑바로	ttok-ba-ro
back (e.g., come ~)	뒤로	dwi-ro
from anywhere	어디에서든지	eo-di-e-seo-deun-ji
from somewhere	어디로부터인지	eo-di-ro-bu-teo-in-ji
firstly (adv)	첫째로	cheot-jjae-ro
secondly (adv)	둘째로	dul-jjae-ro
thirdly (adv)	셋째로	set-jjae-ro
suddenly (adv)	갑자기	gap-ja-gi
at first (in the beginning)	처음에	cheo-eum-e
for the first time	처음으로	cheo-eu-meu-ro
long before ...	··· 오래 전에	... o-rae jeon-e
anew (over again)	다시	da-si
for good (adv)	영원히	yeong-won-hi
never (adv)	절대로	jeol-dae-ro
again (adv)	다시	da-si
now (adv)	이제	i-je
often (adv)	자주	ja-ju
then (adv)	그때	geu-ttae
urgently (quickly)	급히	geu-pi
usually (adv)	보통으로	bo-tong-eu-ro
by the way, ...	그건 그렇고, ···	geu-geon geu-reo-ko, ...
possible (that is ~)	가능한	ga-neung-han
probably (adv)	아마	a-ma
maybe (adv)	어쩌면	eo-jjeo-myeon
besides ...	게다가 ···	ge-da-ga ...
that's why ...	그래서 ···	geu-rae-seo ...
in spite of ...	··· 에도 불구하고	... e-do bul-gu-ha-go
thanks to ...	··· 덕분에	... deok-bun-e
something	무엇인가	mu-eon-nin-ga
anything (something)	무엇이든지	mu-eon-ni-deun-ji
nothing	아무것도	a-mu-geot-do
someone	누구	nu-gu
somebody	누군가	nu-gun-ga
nobody	아무도	a-mu-do
nowhere (a voyage to ~)	아무데도	a-mu-de-do
nobody's	누구의 것도 아닌	nu-gu-ui geot-do a-nin
somebody's	누군가의	nu-gun-ga-ui
so (I'm ~ glad)	그래서	geu-rae-seo

| also (as well) | 역시 | yeok-si |
| too (as well) | 또한 | tto-han |

6. Function words. Adverbs. Part 2

Why?	왜?	wae?
for some reason	어떤 이유로	eo-tteon ni-yu-ro
because ...	왜냐하면 ···	wae-nya-ha-myeon ...
for some purpose	어떤 목적으로	eo-tteon mok-jeo-geu-ro

and	그리고	geu-ri-go
or	또는	tto-neun
but	그러나	geu-reo-na
for (e.g., ~ me)	위해서	wi-hae-seo

too (~ many people)	너무	neo-mu
only (exclusively)	··· 만	... man
exactly (adv)	정확하게	jeong-hwak-a-ge
about (more or less)	약	yak

approximately (adv)	대략	dae-ryak
approximate (adj)	대략적인	dae-ryak-jeo-gin
almost (adv)	거의	geo-ui
the rest	나머지	na-meo-ji

each (adj)	각각의	gak-ga-gui
any (no matter which)	아무	a-mu
many, much (a lot of)	많이	ma-ni
many people	많은 사람들	ma-neun sa-ram-deul
all (everyone)	모두	mo-du

in return for ...	··· 의 교환으로	... ui gyo-hwa-neu-ro
in exchange (adv)	교환으로	gyo-hwa-neu-ro
by hand (made)	수공으로	su-gong-eu-ro
hardly (negative opinion)	거의	geo-ui

probably (adv)	아마	a-ma
on purpose (intentionally)	일부러	il-bu-reo
by accident (adv)	우연히	u-yeon-hi

very (adv)	아주	a-ju
for example (adv)	예를 들면	ye-reul deul-myeon
between	사이에	sa-i-e
among	중에	jung-e
so much (such a lot)	이만큼	i-man-keum
especially (adv)	특히	teuk-i

BOOKS
T&P

NUMBERS.
MISCELLANEOUS

T&P Books Publishing

0 zero	영	yeong
1 one	일	il
2 two	이	i
3 three	삼	sam
4 four	사	sa
5 five	오	o
6 six	육	yuk
7 seven	칠	chil
8 eight	팔	pal
9 nine	구	gu
10 ten	십	sip
11 eleven	십일	si-bil
12 twelve	십이	si-bi
13 thirteen	십삼	sip-sam
14 fourteen	십사	sip-sa
15 fifteen	십오	si-bo
16 sixteen	십육	si-byuk
17 seventeen	십칠	sip-chil
18 eighteen	십팔	sip-pal
19 nineteen	십구	sip-gu
20 twenty	이십	i-sip
21 twenty-one	이십일	i-si-bil
22 twenty-two	이십이	i-si-bi
23 twenty-three	이십삼	i-sip-sam
30 thirty	삼십	sam-sip
31 thirty-one	삼십일	sam-si-bil
32 thirty-two	삼십이	sam-si-bi
33 thirty-three	삼십삼	sam-sip-sam
40 forty	사십	sa-sip
41 forty-one	사십일	sa-si-bil
42 forty-two	사십이	sa-si-bi
43 forty-three	사십삼	sa-sip-sam
50 fifty	오십	o-sip
51 fifty-one	오십일	o-si-bil
52 fifty-two	오십이	o-si-bi
53 fifty-three	오십삼	o-sip-sam
60 sixty	육십	yuk-sip

61 sixty-one	육십일	yuk-si-bil
62 sixty-two	육십이	yuk-si-bi
63 sixty-three	육십삼	yuk-sip-sam
70 seventy	칠십	chil-sip
71 seventy-one	칠십일	chil-si-bil
72 seventy-two	칠십이	chil-si-bi
73 seventy-three	칠십삼	chil-sip-sam
80 eighty	팔십	pal-sip
81 eighty-one	팔십일	pal-si-bil
82 eighty-two	팔십이	pal-si-bi
83 eighty-three	팔십삼	pal-sip-sam
90 ninety	구십	gu-sip
91 ninety-one	구십일	gu-si-bil
92 ninety-two	구십이	gu-si-bi
93 ninety-three	구십삼	gu-sip-sam

8. Cardinal numbers. Part 2

100 one hundred	백	baek
200 two hundred	이백	i-baek
300 three hundred	삼백	sam-baek
400 four hundred	사백	sa-baek
500 five hundred	오백	o-baek
600 six hundred	육백	yuk-baek
700 seven hundred	칠백	chil-baek
800 eight hundred	팔백	pal-baek
900 nine hundred	구백	gu-baek
1000 one thousand	천	cheon
2000 two thousand	이천	i-cheon
3000 three thousand	삼천	sam-cheon
10000 ten thousand	만	man
one hundred thousand	십만	sim-man
million	백만	baeng-man
billion	십억	si-beok

9. Ordinal numbers

first (adj)	첫 번째의	cheot beon-jjae-ui
second (adj)	두 번째의	du beon-jjae-ui
third (adj)	세 번째의	se beon-jjae-ui
fourth (adj)	네 번째의	ne beon-jjae-ui
fifth (adj)	다섯 번째의	da-seot beon-jjae-ui
sixth (adj)	여섯 번째의	yeo-seot beon-jjae-ui

seventh (adj)	일곱 번째의	il-gop beon-jjae-ui
eighth (adj)	여덟 번째의	yeo-deol beon-jjae-ui
ninth (adj)	아홉 번째의	a-hop beon-jjae-ui
tenth (adj)	열 번째의	yeol beon-jjae-ui

T&P BOOKS

COLOURS. UNITS OF MEASUREMENT

T&P Books Publishing

color	색	sae
shade (tint)	색조	saek-jo
hue	색상	saek-sang
rainbow	무지개	mu-ji-gae
white (adj)	흰	huin
black (adj)	검은	geo-meun
gray (adj)	회색의	hoe-sae-gui
green (adj)	초록색의	cho-rok-sae-gui
yellow (adj)	노란	no-ran
red (adj)	빨간	ppal-gan
blue (adj)	파란	pa-ran
light blue (adj)	하늘색의	ha-neul-sae-gui
pink (adj)	분홍색의	bun-hong-sae-gui
orange (adj)	주황색의	ju-hwang-sae-gui
violet (adj)	보라색의	bo-ra-sae-gui
brown (adj)	갈색의	gal-sae-gui
golden (adj)	금색의	geum-sae-gui
silvery (adj)	은색의	eun-sae-gui
beige (adj)	베이지색의	be-i-ji-sae-gui
cream (adj)	크림색의	keu-rim-sae-gui
turquoise (adj)	청록색의	cheong-nok-sae-gui
cherry red (adj)	암적색의	am-jeok-sae-gui
lilac (adj)	연보라색의	yeon-bo-ra-sae-gui
crimson (adj)	진홍색의	jin-hong-sae-gui
light (adj)	밝은	bal-geun
dark (adj)	짙은	ji-teun
bright, vivid (adj)	선명한	seon-myeong-han
colored (pencils)	색의	sae-gui
color (e.g., ~ film)	컬러의	keol-leo-ui
black-and-white (adj)	흑백의	heuk-bae-gui
plain (one-colored)	단색의	dan-sae-gui
multicolored (adj)	다색의	da-sae-gui

11. Units of measurement

weight	무게	mu-ge
length	길이	gi-ri

width	폭, 너비	pok, neo-bi
height	높이	no-pi
depth	깊이	gi-pi
volume	부피	bu-pi
area	면적	myeon-jeok

gram	그램	geu-raem
milligram	밀리그램	mil-li-geu-raem
kilogram	킬로그램	kil-lo-geu-raem
ton	톤	ton
pound	파운드	pa-un-deu
ounce	온스	on-seu

meter	미터	mi-teo
millimeter	밀리미터	mil-li-mi-teo
centimeter	센티미터	sen-ti-mi-teo
kilometer	킬로미터	kil-lo-mi-teo
mile	마일	ma-il

inch	인치	in-chi
foot	피트	pi-teu
yard	야드	ya-deu

square meter	제곱미터	je-gom-mi-teo
hectare	헥타르	hek-ta-reu
liter	리터	ri-teo
degree	도	do
volt	볼트	bol-teu
ampere	암페어	am-pe-eo
horsepower	마력	ma-ryeok

quantity	수량, 양	su-ryang, yang
a little bit of ...	… 조금	… jo-geum
half	절반	jeol-ban
dozen	다스	da-seu
piece (item)	조각	jo-gak

| size | 크기 | keu-gi |
| scale (map ~) | 축척 | chuk-cheok |

minimal (adj)	최소의	choe-so-ui
the smallest (adj)	가장 작은	ga-jang ja-geun
medium (adj)	중간의	jung-gan-ui
maximal (adj)	최대의	choe-dae-ui
the largest (adj)	가장 큰	ga-jang keun

12. Containers

| canning jar (glass ~) | 유리병 | yu-ri-byeong |
| can | 캔, 깡통 | kaen, kkang-tong |

bucket	양동이	yang-dong-i
barrel	통	tong
wash basin (e.g., plastic ~)	대야	dae-ya
tank (100L water ~)	탱크	taeng-keu
hip flask	휴대용 술병	hyu-dae-yong sul-byeong
jerrycan	통	tong
tank (e.g., tank car)	탱크	taeng-keu
mug	머그컵	meo-geu-keop
cup (of coffee, etc.)	컵	keop
saucer	받침 접시	bat-chim jeop-si
glass (tumbler)	유리잔	yu-ri-jan
wine glass	와인글라스	wa-in-geul-la-seu
stock pot (soup pot)	냄비	naem-bi
bottle (~ of wine)	병	byeong
neck (of the bottle, etc.)	병목	byeong-mok
carafe (decanter)	디캔터	di-kaen-teo
pitcher	물병	mul-byeong
vessel (container)	용기	yong-gi
pot (crock, stoneware ~)	항아리	hang-a-ri
vase	화병	hwa-byeong
bottle (perfume ~)	향수병	hyang-su-byeong
vial, small bottle	약병	yak-byeong
tube (of toothpaste)	튜브	tyu-beu
sack (bag)	자루	ja-ru
bag (paper ~, plastic ~)	봉투	bong-tu
pack (of cigarettes, etc.)	갑	gap
box (e.g., shoebox)	박스	bak-seu
crate	상자	sang-ja
basket	바구니	ba-gu-ni

MAIN VERBS

to advise (vt)	조언하다	jo-eon-ha-da
to agree (say yes)	동의하다	dong-ui-ha-da
to answer (vi, vt)	대답하다	dae-da-pa-da
to apologize (vi)	사과하다	sa-gwa-ha-da
to arrive (vi)	도착하다	do-chak-a-da
to ask (~ oneself)	묻다	mut-da
to ask (~ sb to do sth)	부탁하다	bu-tak-a-da
to be afraid	무서워하다	mu-sco-wo-ha-da
to be hungry	배가 고프다	bae-ga go-peu-da
to be interested in ...	... 에 관심을 가지다	... e gwan-si-meul ga-ji-da
to be needed	필요하다	pi-ryo-ha-da
to be surprised	놀라다	nol-la-da
to be thirsty	목마르다	mong-ma-reu-da
to begin (vt)	시작하다	si-jak-a-da
to belong to ...	... 에 속하다	... e sok-a-da
to boast (vi)	자랑하다	ja-rang-ha-da
to break (split into pieces)	깨뜨리다	kkae-tteu-ri-da
to call (~ for help)	부르다, 요청하다	bu-reu-da, yo-cheong-ha-da
can (v aux)	할 수 있다	hal su it-da
to catch (vt)	잡다	jap-da
to change (vt)	바꾸다	ba-kku-da
to choose (select)	선택하다	seon-taek-a-da
to come down (the stairs)	내려오다	nae-ryeo-o-da
to compare (vt)	비교하다	bi-gyo-ha-da
to complain (vi, vt)	불평하다	bul-pyeong-ha-da
to confuse (mix up)	혼동하다	hon-dong-ha-da
to continue (vt)	계속하다	gye-sok-a-da
to control (vt)	제어하다	je-eo-ha-da
to cook (dinner)	요리하다	yo-ri-ha-da
to cost (vt)	값이 ... 이다	gap-si ... i-da
to count (add up)	세다	se-da
to count on ...	... 에 의지하다	... e ui-ji-ha-da
to create (vt)	창조하다	chang-jo-ha-da
to cry (weep)	울다	ul-da

14. The most important verbs. Part 2

to deceive (vi, vt)	속이다	so-gi-da
to decorate (tree, street)	장식하다	jang-sik-a-da
to defend (a country, etc.)	방어하다	bang-eo-ha-da
to demand (request firmly)	요구하다	yo-gu-ha-da
to dig (vt)	파다	pa-da
to discuss (vt)	의논하다	ui-non-ha-da
to do (vt)	하다	ha-da
to doubt (have doubts)	의심하다	ui-sim-ha-da
to drop (let fall)	떨어뜨리다	tteo-reo-tteu-ri-da
to enter (room, house, etc.)	들어가다	deu-reo-ga-da
to exist (vi)	존재하다	jon-jae-ha-da
to expect (foresee)	예상하다	ye-sang-ha-da
to explain (vt)	설명하다	seol-myeong-ha-da
to fall (vi)	떨어지다	tteo-reo-ji-da
to find (vt)	찾다	chat-da
to finish (vt)	끝내다	kkeun-nae-da
to fly (vi)	날다	nal-da
to follow ... (come after)	··· 를 따라가다	... reul tta-ra-ga-da
to forget (vi, vt)	잊다	it-da
to forgive (vt)	용서하다	yong-seo-ha-da
to give (vt)	주다	ju-da
to give a hint	힌트를 주다	hin-teu-reul ju-da
to go (on foot)	가다	ga-da
to go for a swim	수영하다	su-yeong-ha-da
to go out (for dinner, etc.)	나가다	na-ga-da
to guess (the answer)	추측하다	chu-cheuk-a-da
to have (vt)	가지다	ga-ji-da
to have breakfast	아침을 먹다	a-chi-meul meok-da
to have dinner	저녁을 먹다	jeo-nyeo-geul meok-da
to have lunch	점심을 먹다	jeom-si-meul meok-da
to hear (vt)	듣다	deut-da
to help (vt)	도와주다	do-wa-ju-da
to hide (vt)	숨기다	sum-gi-da
to hope (vi, vt)	희망하다	hui-mang-ha-da
to hunt (vi, vt)	사냥하다	sa-nyang-ha-da
to hurry (vi)	서두르다	seo-du-reu-da

15. The most important verbs. Part 3

to inform (vt)	알리다	al-li-da
to insist (vi, vt)	주장하다	ju-jang-ha-da

to insult (vt)	모욕하다	mo-yok-a-da
to invite (vt)	초대하다	cho-dae-ha-da
to joke (vi)	농담하다	nong-dam-ha-da
to keep (vt)	보관하다	bo-gwan-ha-da
to keep silent	침묵을 지키다	chim-mu-geul ji-ki-da
to kill (vt)	죽이다	ju-gi-da
to know (sb)	알다	al-da
to know (sth)	알다	al-da
to laugh (vi)	웃다	ut-da
to liberate (city, etc.)	해방하다	hae-bang-ha-da
to like (I like …)	좋아하다	jo-a-ha-da
to look for … (search)	… 를 찾다	… reul chat-da
to love (sb)	사랑하다	sa-rang-ha-da
to make a mistake	실수하다	sil-su-ha-da
to manage, to run	운영하다	u-nyeong-ha-da
to mean (signify)	의미하다	ui-mi-ha-da
to mention (talk about)	언급하다	eon-geu-pa-da
to miss (school, etc.)	결석하다	gyeol-seok-a-da
to notice (see)	알아차리다	a-ra-cha-ri-da
to object (vi, vt)	반대하다	ban-dae-ha-da
to observe (see)	지켜보다	ji-kyeo-bo-da
to open (vt)	열다	yeol-da
to order (meal, etc.)	주문하다	ju-mun-ha-da
to order (mil.)	명령하다	myeong-nyeong-ha-da
to own (possess)	소유하다	so-yu-ha-da
to participate (vi)	참가하다	cham-ga-ha-da
to pay (vi, vt)	지불하다	ji-bul-ha-da
to permit (vt)	허가하다	heo-ga-ha-da
to plan (vt)	계획하다	gye-hoek-a-da
to play (children)	놀다	nol-da
to pray (vi, vt)	기도하다	gi-do-ha-da
to prefer (vt)	선호하다	seon-ho-ha-da
to promise (vt)	약속하다	yak-sok-a-da
to pronounce (vt)	발음하다	ba-reum-ha-da
to propose (vt)	제안하다	je-an-ha-da
to punish (vt)	처벌하다	cheo-beol-ha-da

16. The most important verbs. Part 4

to read (vi, vt)	읽다	ik-da
to recommend (vt)	추천하다	chu-cheon-ha-da
to refuse (vi, vt)	거절하다	geo-jeol-ha-da
to regret (be sorry)	후회하다	hu-hoe-ha-da
to rent (sth from sb)	임대하다	im-dae-ha-da

to repeat (say again)	반복하다	ban-bok-a-da
to reserve, to book	예약하다	ye-yak-a-da
to run (vi)	달리다	dal-li-da
to save (rescue)	구조하다	gu-jo-ha-da
to say (~ thank you)	말하다	mal-ha-da
to scold (vt)	꾸짖다	kku-jit-da
to see (vt)	보다	bo-da
to sell (vt)	팔다	pal-da
to send (vt)	보내다	bo-nae-da
to shoot (vi)	쏘다	sso-da
to shout (vi)	소리치다	so-ri-chi-da
to show (vt)	보여주다	bo-yeo-ju-da
to sign (document)	서명하다	seo-myeong-ha-da
to sit down (vi)	앉다	an-da
to smile (vi)	미소를 짓다	mi-so-reul jit-da
to speak (vi, vt)	말하다	mal-ha-da
to steal (money, etc.)	훔치다	hum-chi-da
to stop (for pause, etc.)	정지하다	jeong-ji-ha-da
to stop (please ~ calling me)	그만두다	geu-man-du-da
to study (vt)	공부하다	gong-bu-ha-da
to swim (vi)	수영하다	su-yeong-ha-da
to take (vt)	잡다	jap-da
to think (vi, vt)	생각하다	saeng-gak-a-da
to threaten (vt)	협박하다	hyeop-bak-a-da
to touch (with hands)	닿다	da-ta
to translate (vt)	번역하다	beo-nyeok-a-da
to trust (vt)	신뢰하다	sil-loe-ha-da
to try (attempt)	해보다	hae-bo-da
to turn (e.g., ~ left)	돌다	dol-da
to underestimate (vt)	과소평가하다	gwa-so-pyeong-ga-ha-da
to understand (vt)	이해하다	i-hae-ha-da
to unite (vt)	연합하다	yeon-ha-pa-da
to wait (vt)	기다리다	gi-da-ri-da
to want (wish, desire)	원하다	won-ha-da
to warn (vt)	경고하다	gyeong-go-ha-da
to work (vi)	일하다	il-ha-da
to write (vt)	쓰다	sseu-da
to write down	적다	jeok-da

T&P BOOKS

TIME. CALENDAR

T&P Books Publishing

17. Weekdays

Monday	월요일	wo-ryo-il
Tuesday	화요일	hwa-yo-il
Wednesday	수요일	su-yo-il
Thursday	목요일	mo-gyo-il
Friday	금요일	geu-myo-il
Saturday	토요일	to-yo-il
Sunday	일요일	i-ryo-il
today (adv)	오늘	o-neul
tomorrow (adv)	내일	nae-il
the day after tomorrow	모레	mo-re
yesterday (adv)	어제	eo-je
the day before yesterday	그저께	geu-jeo-kke
day	낮	nat
working day	근무일	geun-mu-il
public holiday	공휴일	gong-hyu-il
day off	휴일	hyu-il
weekend	주말	ju-mal
all day long	하루종일	ha-ru-jong-il
the next day (adv)	다음날	da-eum-nal
two days ago	이틀 전	i-teul jeon
the day before	전날	jeon-nal
daily (adj)	일간의	il-ga-nui
every day (adv)	매일	mae-il
week	주	ju
last week (adv)	지난 주에	ji-nan ju-e
next week (adv)	다음 주에	da-eum ju-e
weekly (adj)	주간의	ju-ga-nui
every week (adv)	매주	mae-ju
twice a week	일주일에 두번	il-ju-i-re du-beon
every Tuesday	매주 화요일	mae-ju hwa-yo-il

18. Hours. Day and night

morning	아침	a-chim
in the morning	아침에	a-chim-e
noon, midday	정오	jeong-o
in the afternoon	오후에	o-hu-e
evening	저녁	jeo-nyeok

in the evening	저녁에	jeo-nyeo-ge
night	밤	bam
at night	밤에	bam-e
midnight	자정	ja-jeong

second	초	cho
minute	분	bun
hour	시	si
half an hour	반시간	ban-si-gan
a quarter-hour	십오분	si-bo-bun
fifteen minutes	십오분	si-bo-bun
24 hours	이십사시간	i-sip-sa-si-gan

sunrise	일출	il-chul
dawn	새벽	sae-byeok
early morning	이른 아침	i-reun a-chim
sunset	저녁 노을	jeo-nyeok no-eul

early in the morning	이른 아침에	i-reun a-chim-e
this morning	오늘 아침에	o-neul ra-chim-e
tomorrow morning	내일 아침에	nae-il ra-chim-e

this afternoon	오늘 오후에	o-neul ro-hu-e
in the afternoon	오후에	o-hu-e
tomorrow afternoon	내일 오후에	nae-il ro-hu-e

| tonight (this evening) | 오늘 저녁에 | o-neul jeo-nyeo-ge |
| tomorrow night | 내일 밤에 | nae-il bam-e |

at 3 o'clock sharp	3시 정각에	se-si jeong-ga-ge
about 4 o'clock	4시쯤에	ne-si-jjeu-me
by 12 o'clock	12시까지	yeoldu si-kka-ji

in 20 minutes	20분 안에	isib-bun na-ne
in an hour	한 시간 안에	han si-gan na-ne
on time (adv)	제시간에	je-si-gan-e

a quarter of ...	··· 십오 분	... si-bo bun
within an hour	한 시간 내에	han si-gan nae-e
every 15 minutes	15분 마다	sibo-bun ma-da
round the clock	하루종일	ha-ru-jong-il

19. Months. Seasons

January	일월	i-rwol
February	이월	i-wol
March	삼월	sam-wol
April	사월	sa-wol
May	오월	o-wol
June	유월	yu-wol

July	칠월	chi-rwol
August	팔월	pa-rwol
September	구월	gu-wol
October	시월	si-wol
November	십일월	si-bi-rwol
December	십이월	si-bi-wol

spring	봄	bom
in spring	봄에	bom-e
spring (as adj)	봄의	bom-ui

summer	여름	yeo-reum
in summer	여름에	yeo-reum-e
summer (as adj)	여름의	yeo-reu-mui

fall	가을	ga-eul
in fall	가을에	ga-eu-re
fall (as adj)	가을의	ga-eu-rui

winter	겨울	gyeo-ul
in winter	겨울에	gyeo-u-re
winter (as adj)	겨울의	gyeo-ul

month	월, 달	wol, dal
this month	이번 달에	i-beon da-re
next month	다음 달에	da-eum da-re
last month	지난 달에	ji-nan da-re

a month ago	한달 전에	han-dal jeon-e
in a month (a month later)	한 달 안에	han dal ra-ne
in 2 months (2 months later)	두 달 안에	du dal ra-ne
the whole month	한 달 내내	han dal lae-nae
all month long	한달간 내내	han-dal-gan nae-nae

monthly (~ magazine)	월간의	wol-ga-nui
monthly (adv)	매월, 매달	mae-wol, mae-dal
every month	매달	mae-dal
twice a month	한 달에 두 번	han da-re du beon

year	년	nyeon
this year	올해	ol-hae
next year	내년	nae-nyeon
last year	작년	jang-nyeon

a year ago	일년 전	il-lyeon jeon
in a year	일 년 안에	il lyeon na-ne
in two years	이 년 안에	i nyeon na-ne
the whole year	한 해 전체	han hae jeon-che
all year long	일년 내내	il-lyeon nae-nae
every year	매년	mae-nyeon
annual (adj)	연간의	yeon-ga-nui

annually (adv)	매년	mae-nyeon
4 times a year	일년에 네 번	il-lyeon-e ne beon
date (e.g., today's ~)	날짜	nal-jja
date (e.g., ~ of birth)	월일	wo-ril
calendar	달력	dal-lyeok
half a year	반년	ban-nyeon
six months	육개월	yuk-gae-wol
season (summer, etc.)	계절	gye-jeol
century	세기	se-gi

TRAVEL. HOTEL

USD CAD
EUR CHF
JPY HKD
GBP CNY

RECEPTION

T&P Books Publishing

tourism, travel	관광	gwan-gwang
tourist	관광객	gwan-gwang-gaek
trip, voyage	여행	yeo-haeng
adventure	모험	mo-heom
trip, journey	여행	yeo-haeng
vacation	휴가	hyu-ga
to be on vacation	휴가 중이다	hyu-ga jung-i-da
rest	휴양	hyu-yang
train	기차	gi-cha
by train	기차로	gi-cha-ro
airplane	비행기	bi-haeng-gi
by airplane	비행기로	bi-haeng-gi-ro
by car	자동차로	ja-dong-cha-ro
by ship	배로	bae-ro
luggage	짐, 수하물	jim, su-ha-mul
suitcase	여행 가방	yeo-haeng ga-bang
luggage cart	수하물 카트	su-ha-mul ka-teu
passport	여권	yeo-gwon
visa	비자	bi-ja
ticket	표	pyo
air ticket	비행기표	bi-haeng-gi-pyo
guidebook	여행 안내서	yeo-haeng an-nae-seo
map (tourist ~)	지도	ji-do
area (rural ~)	지역	ji-yeok
place, site	곳	got
exotica (n)	이국	i-guk
exotic (adj)	이국적인	i-guk-jeo-gin
amazing (adj)	놀라운	nol-la-un
group	무리	mu-ri
excursion, sightseeing tour	견학, 관광	gyeon-hak, gwan-gwang
guide (person)	가이드	ga-i-deu

21. Hotel

hotel, inn	호텔	ho-tel
motel	모텔	mo-tel

three-star (~ hotel)	3성급	sam-seong-geub
five-star	5성급	o-seong-geub
to stay (in a hotel, etc.)	머무르다	meo-mu-reu-da

room	객실	gaek-sil
single room	일인실	i-rin-sil
double room	더블룸	deo-beul-lum
to book a room	방을 예약하다	bang-eul rye-yak-a-da

| half board | 하숙 | ha-suk |
| full board | 식사 제공 | sik-sa je-gong |

with bath	욕조가 있는	yok-jo-ga in-neun
with shower	샤워가 있는	sya-wo-ga in-neun
satellite television	위성 텔레비전	wi-seong tel-le-bi-jeon
air-conditioner	에어컨	e-eo-keon
towel	수건	su-geon
key	열쇠	yeol-soe

administrator	관리자	gwal-li-ja
chambermaid	객실 청소부	gaek-sil cheong-so-bu
porter, bellboy	포터	po-teo
doorman	도어맨	do-eo-maen

restaurant	레스토랑	re-seu-to-rang
pub, bar	바	ba
breakfast	아침식사	a-chim-sik-sa
dinner	저녁식사	jeo-nyeok-sik-sa
buffet	뷔페	bwi-pe

| lobby | 로비 | ro-bi |
| elevator | 엘리베이터 | el-li-be-i-teo |

| DO NOT DISTURB | 방해하지 마세요 | bang-hae-ha-ji ma-se-yo |
| NO SMOKING | 금연 | geu-myeon |

22. Sightseeing

monument	기념비	gi-nyeom-bi
fortress	요새	yo-sae
palace	궁전	gung-jeon
castle	성	seong
tower	탑	tap
mausoleum	영묘	yeong-myo

architecture	건축	geon-chuk
medieval (adj)	중세의	jung-se-ui
ancient (adj)	고대의	go-dae-ui
national (adj)	국가의	guk-ga-ui
famous (monument, etc.)	유명한	yu-myeong-han

tourist	관광객	gwan-gwang-gaek
guide (person)	가이드	ga-i-deu
excursion, sightseeing tour	견학, 관광	gyeon-hak, gwan-gwang
to show (vt)	보여주다	bo-yeo-ju-da
to tell (vt)	이야기하다	i-ya-gi-ha-da
to find (vt)	찾다	chat-da
to get lost (lose one's way)	길을 잃다	gi-reul ril-ta
map (e.g., subway ~)	노선도	no-seon-do
map (e.g., city ~)	지도	ji-do
souvenir, gift	기념품	gi-nyeom-pum
gift shop	기념품 가게	gi-nyeom-pum ga-ge
to take pictures	사진을 찍다	sa-ji-neul jjik-da
to have one's picture taken	사진을 찍다	sa-ji-neul jjik-da

T&P BOOKS

TRANSPORTATION

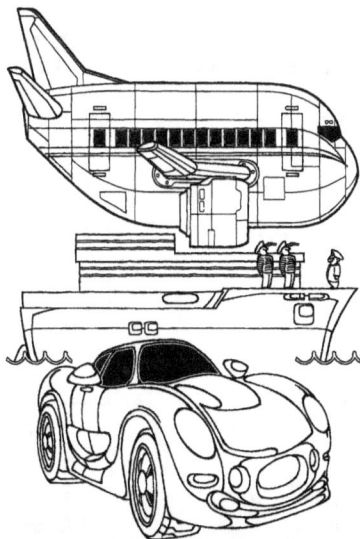

T&P Books Publishing

airport	공항	gong-hang
airplane	비행기	bi-haeng-gi
airline	항공사	hang-gong-sa
air traffic controller	관제사	gwan-je-sa
departure	출발	chul-bal
arrival	도착	do-chak
to arrive (by plane)	도착하다	do-chak-a-da
departure time	출발시간	chul-bal-si-gan
arrival time	도착시간	do-chak-si-gan
to be delayed	연기되다	yeon-gi-doe-da
flight delay	항공기 지연	hang-gong-gi ji-yeon
information board	안내 전광판	an-nae jeon-gwang-pan
information	정보	jeong-bo
to announce (vt)	알리다	al-li-da
flight (e.g., next ~)	비행편	bi-haeng-pyeon
customs	세관	se-gwan
customs officer	세관원	se-gwan-won
customs declaration	세관신고서	se-gwan-sin-go-seo
to fill out the declaration	세관 신고서를 작성하다	se-gwan sin-go-seo-reul jak-seong-ha-da
passport control	여권 검사	yeo-gwon geom-sa
luggage	짐, 수하물	jim, su-ha-mul
hand luggage	휴대 가능 수하물	hyu-dae ga-neung su-ha-mul
luggage cart	수하물 카트	su-ha-mul ka-teu
landing	착륙	chang-nyuk
landing strip	활주로	hwal-ju-ro
to land (vi)	착륙하다	chang-nyuk-a-da
airstairs	승강계단	seung-gang-gye-dan
check-in	체크인	che-keu-in
check-in counter	체크인 카운터	che-keu-in ka-un-teo
to check-in (vi)	체크인하다	che-keu-in-ha-da
boarding pass	탑승권	tap-seung-gwon
departure gate	탑승구	tap-seung-gu
transit	트랜싯, 환승	teu-raen-sit, hwan-seung

to wait (vt)	기다리다	gi-da-ri-da
departure lounge	공항 라운지	gong-hang na-un-ji
to see off	배웅하다	bae-ung-ha-da
to say goodbye	작별인사를 하다	jak-byeo-rin-sa-reul ha-da

24. Airplane

airplane	비행기	bi-haeng-gi
air ticket	비행기표	bi-haeng-gi-pyo
airline	항공사	hang-gong-sa
airport	공항	gong-hang
supersonic (adj)	초음속의	cho-eum-so-gui

pilot	비행사	bi-haeng-sa
flight attendant (fem.)	승무원	seung-mu-won
navigator	항법사	hang-beop-sa

wings	날개	nal-gae
tail	꼬리	kko-ri
cockpit	조종석	jo-jong-seok
engine	엔진	en-jin
undercarriage (landing gear)	착륙 장치	chang-nyuk jang-chi
turbine	터빈	teo-bin

propeller	추진기	chu-jin-gi
black box	블랙박스	beul-laek-bak-seu
yoke (control column)	조종간	jo-jong-gan
fuel	연료	yeol-lyo

safety card	안전 안내서	an-jeon an-nae-seo
oxygen mask	산소 마스크	san-so ma-seu-keu
uniform	제복	je-bok
life vest	구명조끼	gu-myeong-jo-kki
parachute	낙하산	nak-a-san

takeoff	이륙	i-ryuk
to take off (vi)	이륙하다	i-ryuk-a-da
runway	활주로	hwal-ju-ro

visibility	시계	si-gye
flight (act of flying)	비행	bi-haeng
altitude	고도	go-do
air pocket	에어 포켓	e-eo po-ket

seat	자리	ja-ri
headphones	헤드폰	he-deu-pon
folding tray (tray table)	접는 테이블	jeom-neun te-i-beul
airplane window	창문	chang-mun
aisle	통로	tong-no

25. Train

train	기차, 열차	gi-cha, nyeol-cha
commuter train	통근 열차	tong-geun nyeol-cha
express train	급행 열차	geu-paeng yeol-cha
diesel locomotive	디젤 기관차	di-jel gi-gwan-cha
steam locomotive	증기 기관차	jeung-gi gi-gwan-cha
passenger car	객차	gaek-cha
dining car	식당차	sik-dang-cha
rails	레일	re-il
railroad	철도	cheol-do
railway tie	침목	chim-mok
platform (railway ~)	플랫폼	peul-laet-pom
track (~ 1, 2, etc.)	길	gil
semaphore	신호기	sin-ho-gi
station	역	yeok
engineer (train driver)	기관사	gi-gwan-sa
porter (of luggage)	포터	po-teo
car attendant	차장	cha-jang
passenger	승객	seung-gaek
conductor (ticket inspector)	검표원	geom-pyo-won
corridor (in train)	통로	tong-no
emergency brake	비상 브레이크	bi-sang beu-re-i-keu
compartment	침대차	chim-dae-cha
berth	침대	chim-dae
upper berth	윗침대	wit-chim-dae
lower berth	아래 침대	a-rae chim-dae
bed linen, bedding	침구	chim-gu
ticket	표	pyo
schedule	시간표	si-gan-pyo
information display	안내 전광판	an-nae jeon-gwang-pan
to leave, to depart	떠난다	tteo-na-da
departure (of train)	출발	chul-bal
to arrive (ab. train)	도착하다	do-chak-a-da
arrival	도착	do-chak
to arrive by train	기차로 도착하다	gi-cha-ro do-chak-a-da
to get on the train	기차에 타다	gi-cha-e ta-da
to get off the train	기차에서 내리다	gi-cha-e-seo nae-ri-da
train wreck	기차 사고	gi-cha sa-go
steam locomotive	증기 기관차	jeung-gi gi-gwan-cha

stoker, fireman	화부	hwa-bu
firebox	화실	hwa-sil
coal	석탄	seok-tan

26. Ship

| ship | 배 | bae |
| vessel | 배 | bae |

steamship	증기선	jeung-gi-seon
riverboat	강배	gang-bae
cruise ship	크루즈선	keu-ru-jeu-seon
cruiser	순양함	su-nyang-ham

| yacht | 요트 | yo-teu |
| tugboat | 예인선 | ye-in-seon |

| sailing ship | 범선 | beom-seon |
| brigantine | 쌍돛대 범선 | ssang-dot-dae beom-seon |

| ice breaker | 쇄빙선 | swae-bing-seon |
| submarine | 잠수함 | jam-su-ham |

boat (flat-bottomed ~)	보트	bo-teu
dinghy	종선	jong-seon
lifeboat	구조선	gu-jo-seon
motorboat	모터보트	mo-teo-bo-teu

captain	선장	seon-jang
seaman	수부	su-bu
sailor	선원	seon-won
crew	승무원	seung-mu-won

boatswain	갑판장	gap-pan-jang
cook	요리사	yo-ri-sa
ship's doctor	선의	seon-ui

deck	갑판	gap-pan
mast	돛대	dot-dae
sail	돛	dot

hold	화물칸	hwa-mul-kan
bow (prow)	이물	i-mul
stern	고물	go-mul
oar	노	no
screw propeller	스크루	seu-keu-ru

cabin	선실	seon-sil
wardroom	사관실	sa-gwan-sil
engine room	엔진실	en-jin-sil

radio room	무전실	mu-jeon-sil
wave (radio)	전파	jeon-pa
spyglass	망원경	mang-won-gyeong
bell	종	jong
flag	기	gi
hawser (mooring ~)	밧줄	bat-jul
knot (bowline, etc.)	매듭	mae-deup
deckrails	난간	nan-gan
gangway	사다리	sa-da-ri
anchor	닻	dat
to weigh anchor	닻을 올리다	da-cheul rol-li-da
to drop anchor	닻을 내리다	da-cheul lae-ri-da
anchor chain	닻줄	dat-jul
port (harbor)	항구	hang-gu
quay, wharf	부두	bu-du
to berth (moor)	정박시키다	jeong-bak-si-ki-da
to cast off	출항하다	chul-hang-ha-da
trip, voyage	여행	yeo-haeng
cruise (sea trip)	크루즈	keu-ru-jeu
course (route)	항로	hang-no
route (itinerary)	노선	no-seon
fairway	항로	hang-no
(safe water channel)		
shallows	얕은 곳	ya-teun got
to run aground	좌초하다	jwa-cho-ha-da
storm	폭풍우	pok-pung-u
signal	신호	sin-ho
to sink (vi)	가라앉다	ga-ra-an-da
SOS (distress signal)	조난 신호	jo-nan sin-ho
ring buoy	구명부환	gu-myeong-bu-hwan

CITY

T&P Books Publishing

bus	버스	beo-seu
streetcar	전차	jeon-cha
trolley bus	트롤리 버스	teu-rol-li beo-seu
route (of bus, etc.)	노선	no-seon
number (e.g., bus ~)	번호	beon-ho

to go by ...	··· 타고 가다	... ta-go ga-da
to get on (~ the bus)	타다	ta-da
to get off ...	··· 에서 내리다	... e-seo nae-ri-da

stop (e.g., bus ~)	정류장	jeong-nyu-jang
next stop	다음 정류장	da-eum jeong-nyu-jang
terminus	종점	jong-jeom
schedule	시간표	si-gan-pyo
to wait (vt)	기다리다	gi-da-ri-da

| ticket | 표 | pyo |
| fare | 요금 | yo-geum |

cashier (ticket seller)	계산원	gye-san-won
ticket inspection	검표	geom-pyo
ticket inspector	검표원	geom-pyo-won

to be late (for ...)	··· 시간에 늦다	... si-gan-e neut-da
to miss (~ the train, etc.)	놓치다	no-chi-da
to be in a hurry	서두르다	seo-du-reu-da

taxi, cab	택시	taek-si
taxi driver	택시 운전 기사	taek-si un-jeon gi-sa
by taxi	택시로	taek-si-ro
taxi stand	택시 정류장	taek-si jeong-nyu-jang
to call a taxi	택시를 부르다	taek-si-reul bu-reu-da
to take a taxi	택시를 타다	taek-si-reul ta-da

traffic	교통	gyo-tong
traffic jam	교통 체증	gyo-tong che-jeung
rush hour	러시 아워	reo-si a-wo
to park (vi)	주차하다	ju-cha-ha-da
to park (vt)	주차하다	ju-cha-ha-da
parking lot	주차장	ju-cha-jang

subway	지하철	ji-ha-cheol
station	역	yeok
to take the subway	지하철을 타다	ji-ha-cheo-reul ta-da

| train | 기차 | gi-cha |
| train station | 기차역 | gi-cha-yeok |

28. City. Life in the city

city, town	도시	do-si
capital city	수도	su-do
village	마을	ma-eul

city map	도시 지도	do-si ji-do
downtown	시내	si-nae
suburb	근교	geun-gyo
suburban (adj)	근교의	geun-gyo-ui

environs (suburbs)	주변	ju-byeon
city block	한 구획	han gu-hoek
residential block (area)	동	dong

traffic	교통	gyo-tong
traffic lights	신호등	sin-ho-deung
public transportation	대중교통	dae-jung-gyo-tong
intersection	교차로	gyo-cha-ro

crosswalk	횡단 보도	hoeng-dan bo-do
pedestrian underpass	지하 보도	ji-ha bo-do
to cross (~ the street)	건너가다	geon-neo-ga-da
pedestrian	보행자	bo-haeng-ja
sidewalk	인도	in-do

| bridge | 다리 | da-ri |
| embankment (river walk) | 강변로 | gang-byeon-no |

allée (garden walkway)	길	gil
park	공원	gong-won
boulevard	대로	dae-ro
square	광장	gwang-jang
avenue (wide street)	가로	ga-ro
street	거리	geo-ri
side street	골목	gol-mok
dead end	막다른길	mak-da-reun-gil

house	집	jip
building	빌딩	bil-ding
skyscraper	고층 건물	go-cheung geon-mul

facade	전면	jeon-myeon
roof	지붕	ji-bung
window	창문	chang-mun
arch	아치	a-chi
column	기둥	gi-dung

corner	모퉁이	mo-tung-i
store window	쇼윈도우	syo-win-do-u
signboard (store sign, etc.)	간판	gan-pan
poster	포스터	po-seu-teo
advertising poster	광고 포스터	gwang-go po-seu-teo
billboard	광고판	gwang-go-pan
garbage, trash	쓰레기	sseu-re-gi
trashcan (public ~)	쓰레기통	sseu-re-gi-tong
garbage dump	쓰레기장	sseu-re-gi-jang
phone booth	공중 전화	gong-jung jeon-hwa
lamppost	가로등	ga-ro-deung
bench (park ~)	벤치	ben-chi
police officer	경찰관	gyeong-chal-gwan
police	경찰	gyeong-chal
beggar	거지	geo-ji
homeless (n)	노숙자	no-suk-ja

29. Urban institutions

store	가게, 상점	ga-ge, sang-jeom
drugstore, pharmacy	약국	yak-guk
eyeglass store	안경 가게	an-gyeong ga-ge
shopping mall	쇼핑몰	syo-ping-mol
supermarket	슈퍼마켓	syu-peo-ma-ket
bakery	빵집	ppang-jip
baker	제빵사	je-ppang-sa
pastry shop	제과점	je-gwa-jeom
grocery store	식료품점	sing-nyo-pum-jeom
butcher shop	정육점	jeong-yuk-jeom
produce store	야채 가게	ya-chae ga-ge
market	시장	si-jang
coffee house	커피숍	keo-pi-syop
restaurant	레스토랑	re-seu-to-rang
pub, bar	바	ba
pizzeria	피자 가게	pi-ja ga-ge
hair salon	미장원	mi-jang-won
post office	우체국	u-che-guk
dry cleaners	드라이 클리닝	deu-ra-i keul-li-ning
photo studio	사진관	sa-jin-gwan
shoe store	신발 가게	sin-bal ga-ge
bookstore	서점	seo-jeom
sporting goods store	스포츠용품 매장	seu-po-cheu-yong-pum mae-jang

clothes repair shop	옷 수선 가게	ot su-seon ga-ge
formal wear rental	의류 임대	ui-ryu im-dae
video rental store	비디오 대여	bi-di-o dae-yeo
circus	서커스	seo-keo-seu
zoo	동물원	dong-mu-rwon
movie theater	영화관	yeong-hwa-gwan
museum	박물관	bang-mul-gwan
library	도서관	do-seo-gwan
theater	극장	geuk-jang
opera (opera house)	오페라극장	o-pe-ra-geuk-jang
nightclub	나이트 클럽	na-i-teu keul-leop
casino	카지노	ka-ji-no
mosque	모스크	mo-seu-keu
synagogue	유대교 회당	yu-dae-gyo hoe-dang
cathedral	대성당	dae-seong-dang
temple	사원, 신전	sa-won, sin-jeon
church	교회	gyo-hoe
college	단과대학	dan-gwa-dae-hak
university	대학교	dae-hak-gyo
school	학교	hak-gyo
prefecture	도, 현	do, hyeon
city hall	시청	si-cheong
hotel	호텔	ho-tel
bank	은행	eun-haeng
embassy	대사관	dae-sa-gwan
travel agency	여행사	yeo-haeng-sa
information office	안내소	an-nae-so
currency exchange	환전소	hwan-jeon-so
subway	지하철	ji-ha-cheol
hospital	병원	byeong-won
gas station	주유소	ju-yu-so
parking lot	주차장	ju-cha-jang

30. Signs

signboard (store sign, etc.)	간판	gan-pan
notice (door sign, etc.)	안내문	an-nae-mun
poster	포스터	po-seu-teo
direction sign	방향표시	bang-hyang-pyo-si
arrow (sign)	화살표	hwa-sal-pyo
caution	경고	gyeong-go
warning sign	경고판	gyeong-go-pan

to warn (vt)	경고하다	gyeong-go-ha-da
rest day (weekly ~)	휴일	hyu-il
timetable (schedule)	시간표	si-gan-pyo
opening hours	영업 시간	yeong-eop si-gan

WELCOME!	어서 오세요!	eo-seo o-se-yo!
ENTRANCE	입구	ip-gu
EXIT	출구	chul-gu

PUSH	미세요	mi-se-yo
PULL	당기세요	dang-gi-se-yo
OPEN	열림	yeol-lim
CLOSED	닫힘	da-chim

| WOMEN | 여성전용 | yeo-seong-jeo-nyong |
| MEN | 남성 | nam-seong-jeo-nyong |

DISCOUNTS	할인	ha-rin
SALE	세일	se-il
NEW!	신상품	sin-sang-pum
FREE	공짜	gong-jja

ATTENTION!	주의!	ju-ui!
NO VACANCIES	빈 방 없음	bin bang eop-seum
RESERVED	예약석	ye-yak-seok

| ADMINISTRATION | 관리부 | gwal-li-bu |
| STAFF ONLY | 직원 전용 | ji-gwon jeo-nyong |

BEWARE OF THE DOG!	개조심	gae-jo-sim
NO SMOKING	금연	geu-myeon
DO NOT TOUCH!	손 대지 마시오!	son dae-ji ma-si-o!

DANGEROUS	위험	wi-heom
DANGER	위험	wi-heom
HIGH VOLTAGE	고전압	go-jeon-ap
NO SWIMMING!	수영 금지	su-yeong geum-ji
OUT OF ORDER	수리중	su-ri-jung

FLAMMABLE	가연성 물자	ga-yeon-seong mul-ja
FORBIDDEN	금지	geum-ji
NO TRESPASSING!	출입 금지	chu-rip geum-ji
WET PAINT	칠 주의	chil ju-ui

31. Shopping

to buy (purchase)	사다	sa-da
purchase	구매	gu-mae
to go shopping	쇼핑하다	syo-ping-ha-da
shopping	쇼핑	syo-ping

to be open (ab. store)	열리다	yeol-li-da
to be closed	닫다	dat-da
footwear, shoes	신발	sin-bal
clothes, clothing	옷	ot
cosmetics	화장품	hwa-jang-pum
food products	식품	sik-pum
gift, present	선물	seon-mul
salesman	판매원	pan-mae-won
saleswoman	여판매원	yeo-pan-mae-won
check out, cash desk	계산대	gye-san-dae
mirror	거울	geo-ul
counter (store ~)	계산대	gye-san-dae
fitting room	탈의실	ta-rui-sil
to try on	입어보다	i-beo-bo-da
to fit (ab. dress, etc.)	어울리다	eo-ul-li-da
to like (I like …)	좋아하다	jo-a-ha-da
price	가격	ga-gyeok
price tag	가격표	ga-gyeok-pyo
to cost (vt)	값이 … 이다	gap-si … i-da
How much?	얼마?	eol-ma?
discount	할인	ha-rin
inexpensive (adj)	비싸지 않은	bi-ssa-ji a-neun
cheap (adj)	싼	ssan
expensive (adj)	비싼	bi-ssan
It's expensive	비쌉니다	bi-ssam-ni-da
rental (n)	임대	im-dae
to rent (~ a tuxedo)	빌리다	bil-li-da
credit (trade credit)	신용	si-nyong
on credit (adv)	신용으로	si-nyong-eu-ro

T&P BOOKS

CLOTHING & ACCESSORIES

T&P Books Publishing

clothes	옷	ot
outerwear	겉옷	geo-tot
winter clothing	겨울옷	gyeo-u-rot
coat (overcoat)	코트	ko-teu
fur coat	모피 외투	mo-pi oe-tu
fur jacket	짧은 모피 외투	jjal-beun mo-pi oe-tu
down coat	패딩점퍼	pae-ding-jeom-peo
jacket (e.g., leather ~)	재킷	jae-kit
raincoat (trenchcoat, etc.)	트렌치코트	teu-ren-chi-ko-teu
waterproof (adj)	방수의	bang-su-ui

33. Men's & women's clothing

shirt (button shirt)	셔츠	syeo-cheu
pants	바지	ba-ji
jeans	청바지	cheong-ba-ji
suit jacket	재킷	jae-kit
suit	양복	yang-bok
dress (frock)	드레스	deu-re-seu
skirt	치마	chi-ma
blouse	블라우스	beul-la-u-seu
knitted jacket (cardigan, etc.)	니트 재킷	ni-teu jae-kit
jacket (of woman's suit)	재킷	jae-kit
T-shirt	티셔츠	ti-syeo-cheu
shorts (short trousers)	반바지	ban-ba-ji
tracksuit	운동복	un-dong-bok
bathrobe	목욕가운	mo-gyok-ga-un
pajamas	파자마	pa-ja-ma
sweater	스웨터	seu-we-teo
pullover	풀오버	pu-ro-beo
vest	조끼	jo-kki
tailcoat	연미복	yeon-mi-bok
tuxedo	턱시도	teok-si-do
uniform	제복	je-bok
workwear	작업복	ja-geop-bok

| overalls | 작업바지 | ja-geop-ba-ji |
| coat (e.g., doctor's smock) | 가운 | ga-un |

34. Clothing. Underwear

underwear	속옷	so-got
undershirt (A-shirt)	러닝 셔츠	reo-ning syeo-cheu
socks	양말	yang-mal

nightgown	잠옷	jam-ot
bra	브라	beu-ra
knee highs (knee-high socks)	무릎길이 스타킹	mu-reup-gi-ri seu-ta-king
pantyhose	팬티 스타킹	paen-ti seu-ta-king
stockings (thigh highs)	밴드 스타킹	baen-deu seu-ta-king
bathing suit	수영복	su-yeong-bok

35. Headwear

hat	모자	mo-ja
fedora	중절모	jung-jeol-mo
baseball cap	야구 모자	ya-gu mo-ja
flatcap	플랫캡	peul-laet-kaep

beret	베레모	be-re-mo
hood	후드	hu-deu
panama hat	파나마 모자	pa-na-ma mo-ja
knit cap (knitted hat)	니트 모자	ni-teu mo-ja

| headscarf | 스카프 | seu-ka-peu |
| women's hat | 여성용 모자 | yeo-seong-yong mo-ja |

hard hat	안전모	an-jeon-mo
garrison cap	개리슨 캡	gae-ri-seun kaep
helmet	헬멧	hel-met

36. Footwear

footwear	신발	sin-bal
shoes (men's shoes)	구두	gu-du
shoes (women's shoes)	구두	gu-du
boots (e.g., cowboy ~)	부츠	bu-cheu
slippers	슬리퍼	seul-li-peo
tennis shoes (e.g., Nike ~)	운동화	un-dong-hwa
sneakers (e.g., Converse ~)	스니커즈	seu-ni-keo-jeu

sandals	샌들	saen-deul
cobbler (shoe repairer)	구둣방	gu-dut-bang
heel	굽	gup
pair (of shoes)	켤레	kyeol-le
shoestring	끈	kkeun
to lace (vt)	끈을 매다	kkeu-neul mae-da
shoehorn	구둣주걱	gu-dut-ju-geok
shoe polish	구두약	gu-du-yak

37. Personal accessories

gloves	장갑	jang-gap
mittens	벙어리장갑	beong-eo-ri-jang-gap
scarf (muffler)	목도리	mok-do-ri
glasses (eyeglasses)	안경	an-gyeong
frame (eyeglass ~)	안경테	an-gyeong-te
umbrella	우산	u-san
walking stick	지팡이	ji-pang-i
hairbrush	빗, 솔빗	bit, sol-bit
fan	부채	bu-chae
tie (necktie)	넥타이	nek-ta-i
bow tie	나비넥타이	na-bi-nek-ta-i
suspenders	멜빵	mel-ppang
handkerchief	손수건	son-su-geon
comb	빗	bit
barrette	머리핀	meo-ri-pin
hairpin	머리핀	meo-ri-pin
buckle	버클	beo-keul
belt	벨트	bel-teu
shoulder strap	어깨끈	eo-kkae-kkeun
bag (handbag)	가방	ga-bang
purse	핸드백	haen-deu-baek
backpack	배낭	bae-nang

38. Clothing. Miscellaneous

fashion	패션	pae-syeon
in vogue (adj)	유행하는	yu-haeng-ha-neun
fashion designer	패션 디자이너	pae-syeon di-ja-i-neo
collar	옷깃	ot-git
pocket	주머니, 포켓	ju-meo-ni, po-ket

pocket (as adj)	주머니의	ju-meo-ni-ui
sleeve	소매	so-mae
hanging loop	거는 끈	geo-neun kkeun
fly (on trousers)	바지 지퍼	ba-ji ji-peo

zipper (fastener)	지퍼	ji-peo
fastener	조임쇠	jo-im-soe
button	단추	dan-chu
buttonhole	단춧 구멍	dan-chut gu-meong
to come off (ab. button)	떨어지다	tteo-reo-ji-da

to sew (vi, vt)	바느질하다	ba-neu-jil-ha-da
to embroider (vi, vt)	수놓다	su-no-ta
embroidery	자수	ja-su
sewing needle	바늘	ba-neul
thread	실	sil
seam	솔기	sol-gi

to get dirty (vi)	더러워지다	deo-reo-wo-ji-da
stain (mark, spot)	얼룩	eol-luk
to crease, crumple (vi)	구겨지다	gu-gyeo-ji-da
to tear, to rip (vt)	찢다	jjit-da
clothes moth	좀	jom

39. Personal care. Cosmetics

toothpaste	치약	chi-yak
toothbrush	칫솔	chit-sol
to brush one's teeth	이를 닦다	i-reul dak-da

razor	면도기	myeon-do-gi
shaving cream	면도용 크림	myeon-do-yong keu-rim
to shave (vi)	깎다	kkak-da

| soap | 비누 | bi-nu |
| shampoo | 샴푸 | syam-pu |

scissors	가위	ga-wi
nail file	손톱줄	son-top-jul
nail clippers	손톱깎이	son-top-kka-kki
tweezers	족집게	jok-jip-ge

cosmetics	화장품	hwa-jang-pum
face mask	얼굴 마스크	eol-gul ma-seu-keu
manicure	매니큐어	mae-ni-kyu-eo
to have a manicure	매니큐어를 칠하다	mae-ni-kyu-eo-reul chil-ha-da

pedicure	페디큐어	pe-di-kyu-eo
make-up bag	화장품 가방	hwa-jang-pum ga-bang
face powder	분	bun

powder compact	콤팩트	kom-paek-teu
blusher	블러셔	beul-leo-syeo
perfume (bottled)	향수	hyang-su
toilet water (lotion)	화장수	hwa-jang-su
lotion	로션	ro-syeon
cologne	오드콜로뉴	o-deu-kol-lo-nyu
eyeshadow	아이섀도	a-i-syae-do
eyeliner	아이라이너	a-i-ra-i-neo
mascara	마스카라	ma-seu-ka-ra
lipstick	립스틱	rip-seu-tik
nail polish, enamel	매니큐어	mae-ni-kyu-eo
hair spray	헤어 스프레이	he-eo seu-peu-re-i
deodorant	데오도란트	de-o-do-ran-teu
cream	크림	keu-rim
face cream	얼굴 크림	eol-gul keu-rim
hand cream	핸드 크림	haen-deu keu-rim
anti-wrinkle cream	주름제거 크림	ju-reum-je-geo keu-rim
day (as adj)	낮의	na-jui
night (as adj)	밤의	ba-mui
tampon	탐폰	tam-pon
toilet paper (toilet roll)	화장지	hwa-jang-ji
hair dryer	헤어 드라이어	he-eo deu-ra-i-eo

40. Watches. Clocks

watch (wristwatch)	손목 시계	son-mok si-gye
dial	문자반	mun-ja-ban
hand (of clock, watch)	바늘	ba-neul
metal watch band	금속제 시계줄	geum-sok-je si-gye-jul
watch strap	시계줄	si-gye-jul
battery	건전지	geon-jeon-ji
to be dead (battery)	나가다	na-ga-da
to change a battery	배터리를 갈다	bae-teo-ri-reul gal-da
to run fast	빨리 가다	ppal-li ga-da
to run slow	늦게 가다	neut-ge ga-da
wall clock	벽시계	byeok-si-gye
hourglass	모래시계	mo-rae-si-gye
sundial	해시계	hae-si-gye
alarm clock	알람 시계	al-lam si-gye
watchmaker	시계 기술자	si-gye gi-sul-ja
to repair (vt)	수리하다	su-ri-ha-da

T&P BOOKS

EVERYDAY EXPERIENCE

T&P Books Publishing

money	돈	don
currency exchange	환전	hwan-jeon
exchange rate	환율	hwa-nyul
ATM	현금 자동 지급기	hyeon-geum ja-dong ji-geup-gi

| coin | 동전 | dong-jeon |

| dollar | 달러 | dal-leo |
| euro | 유로 | yu-ro |

lira	리라	ri-ra
Deutschmark	마르크	ma-reu-keu
franc	프랑	peu-rang
pound sterling	파운드	pa-un-deu
yen	엔	en

debt	빚	bit
debtor	채무자	chae-mu-ja
to lend (money)	빌려주다	bil-lyeo-ju-da
to borrow (vi, vt)	빌리다	bil-li-da

bank	은행	eun-haeng
account	계좌	gye-jwa
to deposit into the account	계좌에 입금하다	ip-geum-ha-da
to withdraw (vt)	출금하다	chul-geum-ha-da

credit card	신용 카드	si-nyong ka-deu
cash	현금	hyeon-geum
check	수표	su-pyo
to write a check	수표를 끊다	su-pyo-reul kkeun-ta
checkbook	수표책	su-pyo-chaek

wallet	지갑	ji-gap
change purse	동전지갑	dong-jeon-ji-gap
safe	금고	geum-go

heir	상속인	sang-so-gin
inheritance	유산	yu-san
fortune (wealth)	재산, 큰돈	jae-san, keun-don

lease	임대	im-dae
rent (money)	집세	jip-se
to rent (sth from sb)	임대하다	im-dae-ha-da
price	가격	ga-gyeok

| cost | 비용 | bi-yong |
| sum | 액수 | aek-su |

to spend (vt)	쓰다	sseu-da
expenses	출비를	chul-bi-reul
to economize (vi, vt)	절약하다	jeo-ryak-a-da
economical	경제적인	gyeong-je-jeo-gin

to pay (vi, vt)	지불하다	ji-bul-ha-da
payment	지불	ji-bul
change (give the ~)	거스름돈	geo-seu-reum-don

tax	세금	se-geum
fine	벌금	beol-geum
to fine (vt)	벌금을 부과하다	beol-geu-meul bu-gwa-ha-da

42. Post. Postal service

post office	우체국	u-che-guk
mail (letters, etc.)	우편물	u-pyeon-mul
mailman	우체부	u-che-bu
opening hours	영업 시간	yeong-eop si-gan

letter	편지	pyeon-ji
registered letter	등기 우편	deung-gi u-pyeon
postcard	엽서	yeop-seo
telegram	전보	jeon-bo
package (parcel)	소포	so-po
money transfer	송금	song-geum

to receive (vt)	받다	bat-da
to send (vt)	보내다	bo-nae-da
sending	발송	bal-song
address	주소	ju-so
ZIP code	우편 번호	u-pyeon beon-ho
sender	발송인	bal-song-in
receiver	수신인	su-sin-in

| name (first name) | 이름 | i-reum |
| surname (last name) | 성 | seong |

postage rate	요금	yo-geum
standard (adj)	일반의	il-ba-nui
economical (adj)	경제적인	gyeong-je-jeo-gin

weight	무게	mu-ge
to weigh (~ letters)	무게를 달다	mu-ge-reul dal-da
envelope	봉투	bong-tu
postage stamp	우표	u-pyo

43. Banking

bank	은행	eun-haeng
branch (of bank, etc.)	지점	ji-jeom
bank clerk, consultant	행원	haeng-won
manager (director)	지배인	ji-bae-in
bank account	은행계좌	eun-haeng-gye-jwa
account number	계좌 번호	gye-jwa beon-ho
checking account	당좌	dang-jwa
savings account	보통 예금	bo-tong ye-geum
to open an account	계좌를 열다	gye-jwa-reul ryeol-da
to close the account	계좌를 해지하다	gye-jwa-reul hae-ji-ha-da
to deposit into the account	계좌에 입금하다	ip-geum-ha-da
to withdraw (vt)	출금하다	chul-geum-ha-da
deposit	저금	jeo-geum
to make a deposit	입금하다	ip-geum-ha-da
wire transfer	송금	song-geum
to wire, to transfer	송금하다	song-geum-ha-da
sum	액수	aek-su
How much?	얼마?	eol-ma?
signature	서명	seo-myeong
to sign (vt)	서명하다	seo-myeong-ha-da
credit card	신용 카드	si-nyong ka-deu
code (PIN code)	비밀번호	bi-mil-beon-ho
credit card number	신용 카드 번호	si-nyong ka-deu beon-ho
ATM	현금 자동 지급기	hyeon-geum ja-dong ji-geup-gi
check	수표	su-pyo
to write a check	수표를 끊다	su-pyo-reul kkeun-ta
checkbook	수표책	su-pyo-chaek
loan (bank ~)	대출	dae-chul
to apply for a loan	대출 신청하다	dae-chul sin-cheong-ha-da
to get a loan	대출을 받다	dae-chu-reul bat-da
to give a loan	대출하다	dae-chul-ha-da
guarantee	담보	dam-bo

44. Telephone. Phone conversation

telephone	전화	jeon-hwa
cell phone	휴대폰	hyu-dae-pon

answering machine	자동 응답기	ja-dong eung-dap-gi
to call (by phone)	전화하다	jeon-hwa-ha-da
phone call	통화	tong-hwa
to dial a number	번호로 걸다	beon-ho-ro geol-da
Hello!	여보세요!	yeo-bo-se-yo!
to ask (vt)	묻다	mut-da
to answer (vi, vt)	전화를 받다	jeon-hwa-reul bat-da
to hear (vt)	듣다	deut-da
well (adv)	잘	jal
not well (adv)	좋지 않은	jo-chi a-neun
noises (interference)	잡음	ja-beum
receiver	수화기	su-hwa-gi
to pick up (~ the phone)	전화를 받다	jeon-hwa-reul bat-da
to hang up (~ the phone)	전화를 끊다	jeon-hwa-reul kkeun-ta
busy (engaged)	통화 중인	tong-hwa jung-in
to ring (ab. phone)	울리다	ul-li-da
telephone book	전화 번호부	jeon-hwa beon-ho-bu
local (adj)	시내의	si-nae-ui
long distance (~ call)	장거리의	jang-geo-ri-ui
international (adj)	국제적인	guk-je-jeo-gin

45. Cell phone

cell phone	휴대폰	hyu-dae-pon
display	화면	hwa-myeon
button	버튼	beo-teun
SIM card	SIM 카드	SIM ka-deu
battery	건전지	geon-jeon-ji
to be dead (battery)	나가다	na-ga-da
charger	충전기	chung-jeon-gi
menu	메뉴	me-nyu
settings	설정	seol-jeong
tune (melody)	벨소리	bel-so-ri
to select (vt)	선택하다	seon-taek-a-da
calculator	계산기	gye-san-gi
voice mail	자동 응답기	ja-dong eung-dap-gi
alarm clock	알람 시계	al-lam si-gye
contacts	연락처	yeol-lak-cheo
SMS (text message)	문자 메시지	mun-ja me-si-ji
subscriber	가입자	ga-ip-ja

46. Stationery

ballpoint pen	볼펜	bol-pen
fountain pen	만년필	man-nyeon-pil
pencil	연필	yeon-pil
highlighter	형광펜	hyeong-gwang-pen
felt-tip pen	사인펜	sa-in-pen
notepad	공책	gong-chaek
agenda (diary)	수첩	su-cheop
ruler	자	ja
calculator	계산기	gye-san-gi
eraser	지우개	ji-u-gae
thumbtack	압정	ap-jeong
paper clip	클립	keul-lip
glue	접착제	jeop-chak-je
stapler	호치키스	ho-chi-ki-seu
hole punch	펀치	peon-chi
pencil sharpener	연필깎이	yeon-pil-kka-kki

47. Foreign languages

language	언어	eon-eo
foreign language	외국어	oe-gu-geo
to study (vt)	공부하다	gong-bu-ha-da
to learn (language, etc.)	배우다	bae-u-da
to read (vi, vt)	읽다	ik-da
to speak (vi, vt)	말하다	mal-ha-da
to understand (vt)	이해하다	i-hae-ha-da
to write (vt)	쓰다	sseu-da
fast (adv)	빨리	ppal-li
slowly (adv)	천천히	cheon-cheon-hi
fluently (adv)	유창하게	yu-chang-ha-ge
rules	규칙	gyu-chik
grammar	문법	mun-beop
vocabulary	어휘	eo-hwi
phonetics	음성학	eum-seong-hak
textbook	교과서	gyo-gwa-seo
dictionary	사전	sa-jeon
teach-yourself book	자습서	ja-seup-seo
phrasebook	회화집	hoe-hwa-jip
cassette, tape	테이프	te-i-peu

videotape	비디오테이프	bi-di-o-te-i-peu
CD, compact disc	씨디	ssi-di
DVD	디비디	di-bi-di
alphabet	알파벳	al-pa-bet
to spell (vt)	··· 의 철자이다	… ui cheol-ja-i-da
pronunciation	발음	ba-reum
accent	악센트	ak-sen-teu
with an accent	사투리로	sa-tu-ri-ro
without an accent	억양 없이	eo-gyang eop-si
word	단어	dan-eo
meaning	의미	ui-mi
course (e.g., a French ~)	강좌	gang-jwa
to sign up	등록하다	deung-nok-a-da
teacher	강사	gang-sa
translation (process)	번역	beo-nyeok
translation (text, etc.)	번역	beo-nyeok
translator	번역가	beo-nyeok-ga
interpreter	통역가	tong-yeok-ga
polyglot	수개 국어를 말하는 사람	su-gae gu-geo-reul mal-ha-neun sa-ram
memory	기억력	gi-eong-nyeok

MEALS. RESTAURANT

T&P Books Publishing

48. Table setting

spoon	숟가락	sut-ga-rak
knife	나이프	na-i-peu
fork	포크	po-keu
cup (e.g., coffee ~)	컵	keop
plate (dinner ~)	접시	jeop-si
saucer	받침 접시	bat-chim jeop-si
napkin (on table)	냅킨	naep-kin
toothpick	이쑤시개	i-ssu-si-gae

49. Restaurant

restaurant	레스토랑	re-seu-to-rang
coffee house	커피숍	keo-pi-syop
pub, bar	바	ba
tearoom	카페, 티룸	ka-pe, ti-rum
waiter	웨이터	we-i-teo
waitress	웨이트리스	we-i-teu-ri-seu
bartender	바텐더	ba-ten-deo
menu	메뉴판	me-nyu-pan
wine list	와인 메뉴	wa-in me-nyu
to book a table	테이블 예약을 하다	te-i-beul rye-ya-geul ha-da
course, dish	요리, 코스	yo-ri, ko-seu
to order (meal)	주문하다	ju-mun-ha-da
to make an order	주문을 하다	ju-mu-neul ha-da
aperitif	아페리티프	a-pe-ri-ti-peu
appetizer	애피타이저	ae-pi-ta-i-jeo
dessert	디저트	di-jeo-teu
check	계산서	gye-san-seo
to pay the check	계산하다	gye-san-ha-da
to give change	거스름돈을 주다	geo-seu-reum-do-neul ju-da
tip	팁	tip

50. Meals

| food | 음식 | eum-sik |
| to eat (vi, vt) | 먹다 | meok-da |

breakfast	아침식사	a-chim-sik-sa
to have breakfast	아침을 먹다	a-chi-meul meok-da
lunch	점심식사	jeom-sim-sik-sa
to have lunch	점심을 먹다	jeom-si-meul meok-da
dinner	저녁식사	jeo-nyeok-sik-sa
to have dinner	저녁을 먹다	jeo-nyeo-geul meok-da

| appetite | 식욕 | si-gyok |
| Enjoy your meal! | 맛있게 드십시오! | man-nit-ge deu-sip-si-o! |

to open (~ a bottle)	열다	yeol-da
to spill (liquid)	엎지르다	eop-ji-reu-da
to spill out (vi)	쏟아지다	sso-da-ji-da

to boil (vi)	끓다	kkeul-ta
to boil (vt)	끓이다	kkeu-ri-da
boiled (~ water)	끓인	kkeu-rin
to chill, cool down (vt)	식히다	sik-i-da
to chill (vi)	식다	sik-da

| taste, flavor | 맛 | mat |
| aftertaste | 뒷 맛 | dwit mat |

to slim down (lose weight)	살을 빼다	sa-reul ppae-da
diet	다이어트	da-i-eo-teu
vitamin	비타민	bi-ta-min
calorie	칼로리	kal-lo-ri
vegetarian (n)	채식주의자	chae-sik-ju-ui-ja
vegetarian (adj)	채식주의의	chae-sik-ju-ui-ui

fats (nutrient)	지방	ji-bang
proteins	단백질	dan-baek-jil
carbohydrates	탄수화물	tan-su-hwa-mul

slice (of lemon, ham)	조각	jo-gak
piece (of cake, pie)	조각	jo-gak
crumb (of bread, cake, etc.)	부스러기	bu-seu-reo-gi

51. Cooked dishes

course, dish	요리, 코스	yo-ri, ko-seu
cuisine	요리	yo-ri
recipe	요리법	yo-ri-beop

portion	분량	bul-lyang
salad	샐러드	sael-leo-deu
soup	수프	su-peu
clear soup (broth)	육수	yuk-su
sandwich (bread)	샌드위치	saen-deu-wi-chi
fried eggs	계란후라이	gye-ran-hu-ra-i
hamburger (beefburger)	햄버거	haem-beo-geo
beefsteak	비프스테이크	bi-peu-seu-te-i-keu
side dish	사이드 메뉴	sa-i-deu me-nyu
spaghetti	스파게티	seu-pa-ge-ti
mashed potatoes	으깬 감자	eu-kkaen gam-ja
pizza	피자	pi-ja
porridge (oatmeal, etc.)	죽	juk
omelet	오믈렛	o-meul-let
boiled (e.g., ~ beef)	삶은	sal-meun
smoked (adj)	훈제된	hun-je-doen
fried (adj)	튀긴	twi-gin
dried (adj)	말린	mal-lin
frozen (adj)	얼린	eol-lin
pickled (adj)	초절인	cho-jeo-rin
sweet (sugary)	단	dan
salty (adj)	짠	jjan
cold (adj)	차가운	cha-ga-un
hot (adj)	뜨거운	tteu-geo-un
bitter (adj)	쓴	sseun
tasty (adj)	맛있는	man-nin-neun
to cook in boiling water	삶다	sam-da
to cook (dinner)	요리하다	yo-ri-ha-da
to fry (vt)	부치다	bu-chi-da
to heat up (food)	데우다	de-u-da
to salt (vt)	소금을 넣다	so-geu-meul leo-ta
to pepper (vt)	후추를 넣다	hu-chu-reul leo-ta
to grate (vt)	강판에 갈다	gang-pa-ne gal-da
peel (n)	껍질	kkeop-jil
to peel (vt)	껍질 벗기다	kkeop-jil beot-gi-da

52. Food

meat	고기	go-gi
chicken	닭고기	dak-go-gi
Rock Cornish hen (poussin)	영계	yeong-gye
duck	오리고기	o-ri-go-gi

goose	거위고기	geo-wi-go-gi
game	사냥감	sa-nyang-gam
turkey	칠면조고기	chil-myeon-jo-go-gi
pork	돼지고기	dwae-ji-go-gi
veal	송아지 고기	song-a-ji go-gi
lamb	양고기	yang-go-gi
beef	소고기	so-go-gi
rabbit	토끼고기	to-kki-go-gi
sausage (bologna, pepperoni, etc.)	소시지	so-si-ji
vienna sausage (frankfurter)	비엔나 소시지	bi-en-na so-si-ji
bacon	베이컨	be-i-keon
ham	햄	haem
gammon	개먼	gae-meon
pâté	파테	pa-te
liver	간	gan
hamburger (ground beef)	다진 고기	da-jin go-gi
tongue	혀	hyeo
egg	계란	gye-ran
eggs	계란	gye-ran
egg white	흰자	huin-ja
egg yolk	노른자	no-reun-ja
fish	생선	saeng-seon
seafood	해물	hae-mul
caviar	캐비어	kae-bi-eo
crab	게	ge
shrimp	새우	sae-u
oyster	굴	gul
spiny lobster	대하	dae-ha
octopus	문어	mun-eo
squid	오징어	o-jing-eo
sturgeon	철갑상어	cheol-gap-sang-eo
salmon	연어	yeon-eo
halibut	넙치	neop-chi
cod	대구	dae-gu
mackerel	고등어	go-deung-eo
tuna	참치	cham-chi
eel	뱀장어	baem-jang-eo
trout	송어	song-eo
sardine	정어리	jeong-eo-ri
pike	강꼬치고기	gang-kko-chi-go-gi
herring	청어	cheong-eo

bread	빵	ppang
cheese	치즈	chi-jeu
sugar	설탕	seol-tang
salt	소금	so-geum
rice	쌀	ssal
pasta (macaroni)	파스타	pa-seu-ta
noodles	면	myeon
butter	버터	beo-teo
vegetable oil	식물유	sing-mu-ryu
sunflower oil	해바라기유	hae-ba-ra-gi-yu
margarine	마가린	ma-ga-rin
olives	올리브	ol-li-beu
olive oil	올리브유	ol-li-beu-yu
milk	우유	u-yu
condensed milk	연유	yeo-nyu
yogurt	요구르트	yo-gu-reu-teu
sour cream	사워크림	sa-wo-keu-rim
cream (of milk)	크림	keu-rim
mayonnaise	마요네즈	ma-yo-ne-jeu
buttercream	버터크림	beo-teo-keu-rim
cereal grains (wheat, etc.)	곡물	gong-mul
flour	밀가루	mil-ga-ru
canned food	통조림	tong-jo-rim
cornflakes	콘플레이크	kon-peul-le-i-keu
honey	꿀	kkul
jam	잼	jaem
chewing gum	껌	kkeom

53. Drinks

water	물	mul
drinking water	음료수	eum-nyo-su
mineral water	미네랄 워터	mi-ne-ral rwo-teo
still (adj)	탄산 없는	tan-san neom-neun
carbonated (adj)	탄산의	tan-sa-nui
sparkling (adj)	탄산이 든	tan-san-i deun
ice	얼음	eo-reum
with ice	얼음을 넣은	eo-reu-meul leo-eun
non-alcoholic (adj)	무알코올의	mu-al-ko-o-rui
soft drink	청량음료	cheong-nyang-eum-nyo
refreshing drink	청량 음료	cheong-nyang eum-nyo

lemonade	레모네이드	re-mo-ne-i-deu
liquors	술	sul
wine	와인	wa-in
white wine	백 포도주	baek po-do-ju
red wine	레드 와인	re-deu wa-in
liqueur	리큐르	ri-kyu-reu
champagne	샴페인	syam-pe-in
vermouth	베르무트	be-reu-mu-teu
whiskey	위스키	wi-seu-ki
vodka	보드카	bo-deu-ka
gin	진	jin
cognac	코냑	ko-nyak
rum	럼	reom
coffee	커피	keo-pi
black coffee	블랙 커피	beul-laek keo-pi
coffee with milk	밀크 커피	mil-keu keo-pi
cappuccino	카푸치노	ka-pu-chi-no
instant coffee	인스턴트 커피	in-seu-teon-teu keo-pi
milk	우유	u-yu
cocktail	칵테일	kak-te-il
milkshake	밀크 셰이크	mil-keu sye-i-keu
juice	주스	ju-seu
tomato juice	토마토 주스	to-ma-to ju-seu
orange juice	오렌지 주스	o-ren-ji ju-seu
freshly squeezed juice	생과일주스	saeng-gwa-il-ju-seu
beer	맥주	maek-ju
light beer	라거	ra-geo
dark beer	흑맥주	heung-maek-ju
tea	차	cha
black tea	홍차	hong-cha
green tea	녹차	nok-cha

54. Vegetables

vegetables	채소	chae-so
greens	녹황색 채소	nok-wang-saek chae-so
tomato	토마토	to-ma-to
cucumber	오이	o-i
carrot	당근	dang-geun
potato	감자	gam-ja
onion	양파	yang-pa
garlic	마늘	ma-neul

cabbage	양배추	yang-bae-chu
cauliflower	컬리플라워	keol-li-peul-la-wo
Brussels sprouts	방울다다기 양배추	bang-ul-da-da-gi yang-bae-chu
broccoli	브로콜리	beu-ro-kol-li

beetroot	비트	bi-teu
eggplant	가지	ga-ji
zucchini	애호박	ae-ho-bak
pumpkin	호박	ho-bak
turnip	순무	sun-mu

parsley	파슬리	pa-seul-li
dill	딜	dil
lettuce	양상추	yang-sang-chu
celery	셀러리	sel-leo-ri
asparagus	아스파라거스	a-seu-pa-ra-geo-seu
spinach	시금치	si-geum-chi

pea	완두	wan-du
beans	콩	kong
corn (maize)	옥수수	ok-su-su
kidney bean	강낭콩	gang-nang-kong

bell pepper	피망	pi-mang
radish	무	mu
artichoke	아티초크	a-ti-cho-keu

55. Fruits. Nuts

fruit	과일	gwa-il
apple	사과	sa-gwa
pear	배	bae
lemon	레몬	re-mon
orange	오렌지	o-ren-ji
strawberry (garden ~)	딸기	ttal-gi

mandarin	귤	gyul
plum	자두	ja-du
peach	복숭아	bok-sung-a
apricot	살구	sal-gu
raspberry	라즈베리	ra-jeu-be-ri
pineapple	파인애플	pa-in-ae-peul

banana	바나나	ba-na-na
watermelon	수박	su-bak
grape	포도	po-do
sour cherry	신양	si-nyang
sweet cherry	양벚나무	yang-beon-na-mu
melon	멜론	mel-lon

grapefruit	자몽	ja-mong
avocado	아보카도	a-bo-ka-do
papaya	파파야	pa-pa-ya
mango	망고	mang-go
pomegranate	석류	seong-nyu

redcurrant	레드커렌트	re-deu-keo-ren-teu
blackcurrant	블랙커렌트	beul-laek-keo-ren-teu
gooseberry	구스베리	gu-seu-be-ri
bilberry	빌베리	bil-be-ri
blackberry	블랙베리	beul-laek-be-ri

raisin	건포도	geon-po-do
fig	무화과	mu-hwa-gwa
date	대추야자	dae-chu-ya-ja

peanut	땅콩	ttang-kong
almond	아몬드	a-mon-deu
walnut	호두	ho-du
hazelnut	개암	gae-am
coconut	코코넛	ko-ko-neot
pistachios	피스타치오	pi-seu-ta-chi-o

56. Bread. Candy

bakers' confectionery (pastry)	과자류	gwa-ja-ryu
bread	빵	ppang
cookies	쿠키	ku-ki

chocolate (n)	초콜릿	cho-kol-lit
chocolate (as adj)	초콜릿의	cho-kol-lis-ui
candy (wrapped)	사탕	sa-tang
cake (e.g., cupcake)	케이크	ke-i-keu
cake (e.g., birthday ~)	케이크	ke-i-keu

| pie (e.g., apple ~) | 파이 | pa-i |
| filling (for cake, pie) | 속 | sok |

jam (whole fruit jam)	잼	jaem
marmalade	마멀레이드	ma-meol-le-i-deu
waffles	와플	wa-peul
ice-cream	아이스크림	a-i-seu-keu-rim

57. Spices

| salt | 소금 | so-geum |
| salty (adj) | 짜 | jja |

to salt (vt)	소금을 넣다	so-geu-meul leo-ta
black pepper	후추	hu-chu
red pepper (milled ~)	고춧가루	go-chut-ga-ru
mustard	겨자	gyeo-ja
horseradish	고추냉이	go-chu-naeng-i
condiment	양념	yang-nyeom
spice	향료	hyang-nyo
sauce	소스	so-seu
vinegar	식초	sik-cho
anise	아니스	a-ni-seu
basil	바질	ba-jil
cloves	정향	jeong-hyang
ginger	생강	saeng-gang
coriander	고수	go-su
cinnamon	계피	gye-pi
sesame	깨	kkae
bay leaf	월계수잎	wol-gye-su-ip
paprika	파프리카	pa-peu-ri-ka
caraway	캐러웨이	kae-reo-we-i
saffron	사프란	sa-peu-ran

T&P BOOKS

PERSONAL
INFORMATION. FAMILY

T&P Books Publishing

name (first name)	이름	i-reum
surname (last name)	성	seong
date of birth	생년월일	saeng-nyeon-wo-ril
place of birth	탄생지	tan-saeng-ji
nationality	국적	guk-jeok
place of residence	거소	geo-so
country	나라	na-ra
profession (occupation)	직업	ji-geop
gender, sex	성별	seong-byeol
height	키	ki
weight	몸무게	mom-mu-ge

59. Family members. Relatives

mother	어머니	eo-meo-ni
father	아버지	a-beo-ji
son	아들	a-deul
daughter	딸	ttal
younger daughter	작은딸	ja-geun-ttal
younger son	작은아들	ja-geun-a-deul
eldest daughter	맏딸	mat-ttal
eldest son	맏아들	ma-da-deul
brother	형제	hyeong-je
sister	자매	ja-mae
cousin (masc.)	사촌 형제	sa-chon hyeong-je
cousin (fem.)	사촌 자매	sa-chon ja-mae
mom, mommy	엄마	eom-ma
dad, daddy	아빠	a-ppa
parents	부모	bu-mo
child	아이, 아동	a-i, a-dong
children	아이들	a-i-deul
grandmother	할머니	hal-meo-ni
grandfather	할아버지	ha-ra-beo-ji
grandson	손자	son-ja
granddaughter	손녀	son-nyeo

grandchildren	손자들	son-ja-deul
uncle	삼촌	sam-chon
nephew	조카	jo-ka
niece	조카딸	jo-ka-ttal

mother-in-law (wife's mother)	장모	jang-mo
father-in-law (husband's father)	시아버지	si-a-beo-ji
son-in-law (daughter's husband)	사위	sa-wi
stepmother	계모	gye-mo
stepfather	계부	gye-bu

infant	영아	yeong-a
baby (infant)	아기	a-gi
little boy, kid	꼬마	kko-ma

wife	아내	a-nae
husband	남편	nam-pyeon
spouse (husband)	배우자	bae-u-ja
spouse (wife)	배우자	bae-u-ja

married (masc.)	결혼한	gyeol-hon-han
married (fem.)	결혼한	gyeol-hon-han
single (unmarried)	미혼의	mi-hon-ui
bachelor	미혼 남자	mi-hon nam-ja
divorced (masc.)	이혼한	i-hon-han
widow	과부	gwa-bu
widower	홀아비	ho-ra-bi

relative	친척	chin-cheok
close relative	가까운 친척	ga-kka-un chin-cheok
distant relative	먼 친척	meon chin-cheok
relatives	친척들	chin-cheok-deul

orphan (boy or girl)	고아	go-a
guardian (of a minor)	후견인	hu-gyeon-in
to adopt (a boy)	입양하다	i-byang-ha-da
to adopt (a girl)	입양하다	i-byang-ha-da

60. Friends. Coworkers

friend (masc.)	친구	chin-gu
friend (fem.)	친구	chin-gu
friendship	우정	u-jeong
to be friends	사귀다	sa-gwi-da

| buddy (masc.) | 벗 | beot |
| buddy (fem.) | 벗 | beot |

partner	파트너	pa-teu-neo
chief (boss)	상사	sang-sa
superior (n)	윗사람	wit-sa-ram
subordinate (n)	부하	bu-ha
colleague	동료	dong-nyo
acquaintance (person)	아는 사람	a-neun sa-ram
fellow traveler	동행자	dong-haeng-ja
classmate	동급생	dong-geup-saeng
neighbor (masc.)	이웃	i-ut
neighbor (fem.)	이웃	i-ut
neighbors	이웃들	i-ut-deul

HUMAN BODY. MEDICINE

T&P Books Publishing

head	머리	meo-ri
face	얼굴	eol-gul
nose	코	ko
mouth	입	ip

eye	눈	nun
eyes	눈	nun
pupil	눈동자	nun-dong-ja
eyebrow	눈썹	nun-sseop
eyelash	속눈썹	sog-nun-sseop
eyelid	눈꺼풀	nun-kkeo-pul

tongue	혀	hyeo
tooth	이	i
lips	입술	ip-sul
cheekbones	광대뼈	gwang-dae-ppyeo
gum	잇몸	in-mom
palate	입천장	ip-cheon-jang

nostrils	콧구멍	kot-gu-meong
chin	턱	teok
jaw	턱	teok
cheek	뺨, 볼	ppyam, bol

forehead	이마	i-ma
temple	관자놀이	gwan-ja-no-ri
ear	귀	gwi
back of the head	뒤통수	dwi-tong-su
neck	목	mok
throat	목구멍	mok-gu-meong

hair	머리털, 헤어	meo-ri-teol, he-eo
hairstyle	머리 스타일	meo-ri seu-ta-il
haircut	헤어컷	he-eo-keot
wig	가발	ga-bal

mustache	콧수염	kot-su-yeom
beard	턱수염	teok-su-yeom
to have (a beard, etc.)	기르다	gi-reu-da
braid	땋은 머리	tta-eun meo-ri
sideburns	구레나룻	gu-re-na-rut

red-haired (adj)	빨강머리의	ppal-gang-meo-ri-ui
gray (hair)	흰머리의	huin-meo-ri-ui

bald (adj)	대머리인	dae-meo-ri-in
bald patch	땜통	ttaem-tong
ponytail	말총머리	mal-chong-meo-ri
bangs	앞머리	am-meo-ri

62. Human body

hand	손	son
arm	팔	pal
finger	손가락	son-ga-rak
thumb	엄지손가락	eom-ji-son-ga-rak
little finger	새끼손가락	sae-kki-son-ga-rak
nail	손톱	son-top
fist	주먹	ju-meok
palm	손바닥	son-ba-dak
wrist	손목	son-mok
forearm	전박	jeon-bak
elbow	팔꿈치	pal-kkum-chi
shoulder	어깨	eo-kkae
leg	다리	da-ri
foot	발	bal
knee	무릎	mu-reup
calf (part of leg)	종아리	jong-a-ri
hip	엉덩이	eong-deong-i
heel	발뒤꿈치	bal-dwi-kkum-chi
body	몸	mom
stomach	배	bae
chest	가슴	ga-seum
breast	가슴	ga-seum
flank	옆구리	yeop-gu-ri
back	등	deung
lower back	허리	heo-ri
waist	허리	heo-ri
navel (belly button)	배꼽	bae-kkop
buttocks	엉덩이	eong-deong-i
bottom	엉덩이	eong-deong-i
beauty mark	점	jeom
birthmark	모반	mo-ban
(café au lait spot)		
tattoo	문신	mun-sin
scar	흉터	hyung-teo

63. Diseases

sickness	병	byeong
to be sick	눕다	nup-da
health	건강	geon-gang

runny nose (coryza)	비염	bi-yeom
tonsillitis	편도염	pyeon-do-yeom
cold (illness)	감기	gam-gi
to catch a cold	감기에 걸리다	gam-gi-e geol-li-da

bronchitis	기관지염	gi-gwan-ji-yeom
pneumonia	폐렴	pye-ryeom
flu, influenza	독감	dok-gam

nearsighted (adj)	근시의	geun-si-ui
farsighted (adj)	원시의	won-si-ui
strabismus (crossed eyes)	사시	sa-si
cross-eyed (adj)	사시인	sa-si-in
cataract	백내장	baeng-nae-jang
glaucoma	녹내장	nong-nae-jang

stroke	뇌졸중	noe-jol-jung
heart attack	심장마비	sim-jang-ma-bi
myocardial infarction	심근경색증	sim-geun-gyeong-saek-jeung

| paralysis | 마비 | ma-bi |
| to paralyze (vt) | 마비되다 | ma-bi-doe-da |

allergy	알레르기	al-le-reu-gi
asthma	천식	cheon-sik
diabetes	당뇨병	dang-nyo-byeong

| toothache | 치통, 이앓이 | chi-tong, i-a-ri |
| caries | 충치 | chung-chi |

diarrhea	설사	seol-sa
constipation	변비증	byeon-bi-jeung
stomach upset	배탈	bae-tal
food poisoning	식중독	sik-jung-dok
to get food poisoning	식중독에 걸리다	sik-jung-do-ge geol-li-da

arthritis	관절염	gwan-jeo-ryeom
rickets	구루병	gu-ru-byeong
rheumatism	류머티즘	ryu-meo-ti-jeum

gastritis	위염	wi-yeom
appendicitis	맹장염	maeng-jang-yeom
cholecystitis	담낭염	dam-nang-yeom
ulcer	궤양	gwe-yang
measles	홍역	hong-yeok

rubella (German measles)	풍진	pung-jin
jaundice	황달	hwang-dal
hepatitis	간염	gan-nyeom

schizophrenia	정신 분열증	jeong-sin bu-nyeol-jeung
rabies (hydrophobia)	광견병	gwang-gyeon-byeong
neurosis	신경증	sin-gyeong-jeung
concussion	뇌진탕	noe-jin-tang

cancer	암	am
sclerosis	경화증	gyeong-hwa-jeung
multiple sclerosis	다발성 경화증	da-bal-seong gyeong-hwa-jeung

alcoholism	알코올 중독	al-ko-ol jung-dok
alcoholic (n)	알코올 중독자	al-ko-ol jung-dok-ja
syphilis	매독	mae-dok
AIDS	에이즈	e-i-jeu

tumor	종양	jong-yang
malignant (adj)	악성의	ak-seong-ui
benign (adj)	양성의	yang-seong-ui

fever	열병	yeol-byeong
malaria	말라리아	mal-la-ri-a
gangrene	괴저	goe-jeo
seasickness	뱃멀미	baen-meol-mi
epilepsy	간질	gan-jil

epidemic	유행병	yu-haeng-byeong
typhus	발진티푸스	bal-jin-ti-pu-seu
tuberculosis	결핵	gyeol-haek
cholera	콜레라	kol-le-ra
plague (bubonic ~)	페스트	pe-seu-teu

64. Symptoms. Treatments. Part 1

symptom	증상	jeung-sang
temperature	체온	che-on
high temperature (fever)	열	yeol
pulse	맥박	maek-bak

dizziness (vertigo)	현기증	hyeon-gi-jeung
hot (adj)	뜨거운	tteu-geo-un
shivering	전율	jeo-nyul
pale (e.g., ~ face)	창백한	chang-baek-an

cough	기침	gi-chim
to cough (vi)	기침을 하다	gi-chi-meul ha-da
to sneeze (vi)	재채기하다	jae-chae-gi-ha-da

| faint | 실신 | sil-sin |
| to faint (vi) | 실신하다 | sil-sin-ha-da |

bruise (hématome)	멍	meong
bump (lump)	혹	hok
to bang (bump)	부딪치다	bu-dit-chi-da
contusion (bruise)	타박상	ta-bak-sang
to get a bruise	타박상을 입다	ta-bak-sang-eul rip-da

to limp (vi)	절다	jeol-da
dislocation	탈구	tal-gu
to dislocate (vt)	탈구하다	tal-gu-ha-da
fracture	골절	gol-jeol
to have a fracture	골절하다	gol-jeol-ha-da

cut (e.g., paper ~)	베인	be-in
to cut oneself	베다	jeol-chang-eul rip-da
bleeding	출혈	chul-hyeol

| burn (injury) | 화상 | hwa-sang |
| to get burned | 데다 | de-da |

to prick (vt)	찌르다	jji-reu-da
to prick oneself	찔리다	jjil-li-da
to injure (vt)	다치다	da-chi-da
injury	부상	bu-sang
wound	부상	bu-sang
trauma	정신적 외상	jeong-sin-jeok goe-sang

to be delirious	망상을 껴다	mang-sang-eul gyeok-da
to stutter (vi)	말을 더듬다	ma-reul deo-deum-da
sunstroke	일사병	il-sa-byeong

65. Symptoms. Treatments. Part 2

| pain, ache | 통증 | tong-jeung |
| splinter (in foot, etc.) | 가시 | ga-si |

sweat (perspiration)	땀	ttam
to sweat (perspire)	땀이 나다	ttam-i na-da
vomiting	구토	gu-to
convulsions	경련	gyeong-nyeon

pregnant (adj)	임신한	im-sin-han
to be born	태어나다	tae-eo-na-da
delivery, labor	출산	chul-san
to deliver (~ a baby)	낳다	na-ta
abortion	낙태	nak-tae
breathing, respiration	호흡	ho-heup
in-breath (inhalation)	들숨	deul-sum

out-breath (exhalation)	날숨	nal-sum
to exhale (breathe out)	내쉬다	nae-swi-da
to inhale (vi)	들이쉬다	deu-ri-swi-da

disabled person	장애인	jang-ae-in
cripple	병신	byeong-sin
drug addict	마약 중독자	ma-yak jung-dok-ja

deaf (adj)	귀가 먼	gwi-ga meon
mute (adj)	벙어리인	beong-eo-ri-in
deaf mute (adj)	농아인	nong-a-in

mad, insane (adj)	미친	mi-chin
madman (demented person)	광인	gwang-in
madwoman	광인	gwang-in
to go insane	미치다	mi-chi-da

gene	유전자	yu-jeon-ja
immunity	면역성	myeo-nyeok-seong
hereditary (adj)	유전의	yu-jeon-ui
congenital (adj)	선천적인	seon-cheon-jeo-gin

virus	바이러스	ba-i-reo-seu
microbe	미생물	mi-saeng-mul
bacterium	세균	se-gyun
infection	감염	gam-nyeom

66. Symptoms. Treatments. Part 3

| hospital | 병원 | byeong-won |
| patient | 환자 | hwan-ja |

diagnosis	진단	jin-dan
cure	치료	chi-ryo
to get treatment	치료를 받다	chi-ryo-reul bat-da
to treat (~ a patient)	치료하다	chi-ryo-ha-da
to nurse (look after)	간호하다	gan-ho-ha-da
care (nursing ~)	간호	gan-ho

operation, surgery	수술	su-sul
to bandage (head, limb)	붕대를 감다	bung-dae-reul gam-da
bandaging	붕대	bung-dae

vaccination	예방주사	ye-bang-ju-sa
to vaccinate (vt)	접종하다	jeop-jong-ha-da
injection, shot	주사	ju-sa
to give an injection	주사하다	ju-sa-ha-da
amputation	절단	jeol-dan
to amputate (vt)	절단하다	jeol-dan-ha-da

coma	혼수 상태	hon-su sang-tae
to be in a coma	혼수 상태에 있다	hon-su sang-tae-e it-da
intensive care	집중 치료	jip-jung chi-ryo
to recover (~ from flu)	회복하다	hoe-bok-a-da
condition (patient's ~)	상태	sang-tae
consciousness	의식	ui-sik
memory (faculty)	기억	gi-eok
to pull out (tooth)	빼다	ppae-da
filling	충전물	chung-jeon-mul
to fill (a tooth)	때우다	ttae-u-da
hypnosis	최면	choe-myeon
to hypnotize (vt)	최면을 걸다	choe-myeo-neul geol-da

67. Medicine. Drugs. Accessories

medicine, drug	약	yak
remedy	약제	yak-je
prescription	처방	cheo-bang
tablet, pill	정제	jeong-je
ointment	연고	yeon-go
ampule	앰풀	aem-pul
mixture	혼합물	hon-ham-mul
syrup	물약	mul-lyak
pill	알약	a-ryak
powder	가루약	ga-ru-yak
gauze bandage	거즈 붕대	geo-jeu bung-dae
cotton wool	솜	som
iodine	요오드	yo-o-deu
Band-Aid	반창고	ban-chang-go
eyedropper	점안기	jeom-an-gi
thermometer	체온계	che-on-gye
syringe	주사기	ju-sa-gi
wheelchair	휠체어	hwil-che-eo
crutches	목발	mok-bal
painkiller	진통제	jin-tong-je
laxative	완하제	wan-ha-je
spirits (ethanol)	알코올	al-ko-ol
medicinal herbs	약초	yak-cho
herbal (~ tea)	약초의	yak-cho-ui

T&P BOOKS

APARTMENT

T&P Books Publishing

68. Apartment

apartment	아파트	a-pa-teu
room	방	bang
bedroom	침실	chim-sil
dining room	식당	sik-dang
living room	거실	geo-sil
study (home office)	서재	seo-jae
entry room	곁방	gyeot-bang
bathroom (room with a bath or shower)	욕실	yok-sil
half bath	화장실	hwa-jang-sil
ceiling	천장	cheon-jang
floor	마루	ma-ru
corner	구석	gu-seok

69. Furniture. Interior

furniture	가구	ga-gu
table	식탁, 테이블	sik-tak, te-i-beul
chair	의자	ui-ja
bed	침대	chim-dae
couch, sofa	소파	so-pa
armchair	안락 의자	al-lak gui-ja
bookcase	책장	chaek-jang
shelf	책꽂이	chaek-kko-ji
wardrobe	옷장	ot-jang
coat rack (wall-mounted ~)	옷걸이	ot-geo-ri
coat stand	스탠드옷걸이	seu-taen-deu-ot-geo-ri
bureau, dresser	서랍장	seo-rap-jang
coffee table	커피 테이블	keo-pi te-i-beul
mirror	거울	geo-ul
carpet	양탄자	yang-tan-ja
rug, small carpet	러그	reo-geu
fireplace	벽난로	byeong-nan-no
candle	초	cho
candlestick	촛대	chot-dae

drapes	커튼	keo-teun
wallpaper	벽지	byeok-ji
blinds (jalousie)	블라인드	beul-la-in-deu

table lamp	테이블 램프	deung
wall lamp (sconce)	벽등	byeok-deung
floor lamp	플로어 스탠드	peul-lo-eo seu-taen-deu
chandelier	샹들리에	syang-deul-li-e

leg (of chair, table)	다리	da-ri
armrest	팔걸이	pal-geo-ri
back (backrest)	등받이	deung-ba-ji
drawer	서랍	seo-rap

70. Bedding

bedclothes	침구	chim-gu
pillow	베개	be-gae
pillowcase	베갯잇	be-gaen-nit
duvet, comforter	이불	i-bul
sheet	시트	si-teu
bedspread	침대보	chim-dae-bo

71. Kitchen

kitchen	부엌	bu-eok
gas	가스	ga-seu
gas stove (range)	가스 레인지	ga-seu re-in-ji
electric stove	전기 레인지	jeon-gi re-in-ji
oven	오븐	o-beun
microwave oven	전자 레인지	jeon-ja re-in-ji

refrigerator	냉장고	naeng-jang-go
freezer	냉동고	naeng-dong-go
dishwasher	식기 세척기	sik-gi se-cheok-gi

meat grinder	고기 분쇄기	go-gi bun-swae-gi
juicer	과즙기	gwa-jeup-gi
toaster	토스터	to-seu-teo
mixer	믹서기	mik-seo-gi

coffee machine	커피 메이커	keo-pi me-i-keo
coffee pot	커피 주전자	keo-pi ju-jeon-ja
coffee grinder	커피 그라인더	keo-pi geu-ra-in-deo

kettle	주전자	ju-jeon-ja
teapot	티팟	ti-pat
lid	뚜껑	ttu-kkeong

tea strainer	차거름망	cha-geo-reum-mang
spoon	숟가락	sut-ga-rak
teaspoon	티스푼	ti-seu-pun
soup spoon	숟가락	sut-ga-rak
fork	포크	po-keu
knife	칼	kal

tableware (dishes)	식기	sik-gi
plate (dinner ~)	접시	jeop-si
saucer	받침 접시	bat-chim jeop-si

shot glass	소주잔	so-ju-jan
glass (tumbler)	유리잔	yu-ri-jan
cup	컵	keop

sugar bowl	설탕그릇	seol-tang-geu-reut
salt shaker	소금통	so-geum-tong
pepper shaker	후추통	hu-chu-tong
butter dish	버터 접시	beo-teo jeop-si

stock pot (soup pot)	냄비	naem-bi
frying pan (skillet)	프라이팬	peu-ra-i-paen
ladle	국자	guk-ja
colander	체	che
tray (serving ~)	쟁반	jaeng-ban

bottle	병	byeong
jar (glass)	유리병	yu-ri-byeong
can	캔, 깡통	kaen, kkang-tong

bottle opener	병따개	byeong-tta-gae
can opener	깡통 따개	kkang-tong tta-gae
corkscrew	코르크 마개 뽑이	ko-reu-keu ma-gae ppo-bi
filter	필터	pil-teo
to filter (vt)	여과하다	yeo-gwa-ha-da

trash, garbage (food waste, etc.)	쓰레기	sseu-re-gi
trash can (kitchen ~)	쓰레기통	sseu-re-gi-tong

72. Bathroom

bathroom	욕실	yok-sil
water	물	mul
faucet	수도꼭지	su-do-kkok-ji
hot water	온수	on-su
cold water	냉수	naeng-su

toothpaste	치약	chi-yak
to brush one's teeth	이를 닦다	i-reul dak-da

to shave (vi)	깎다	kkak-da
shaving foam	면도 크림	myeon-do keu-rim
razor	면도기	myeon-do-gi

to wash (one's hands, etc.)	씻다	ssit-da
to take a bath	목욕하다	mo-gyok-a-da
shower	샤워	sya-wo
to take a shower	샤워하다	sya-wo-ha-da

bathtub	욕조	yok-jo
toilet (toilet bowl)	변기	byeon-gi
sink (washbasin)	세면대	se-myeon-dae

| soap | 비누 | bi-nu |
| soap dish | 비누 그릇 | bi-nu geu-reut |

sponge	스펀지	seu-peon-ji
shampoo	샴푸	syam-pu
towel	수건	su-geon
bathrobe	목욕가운	mo-gyok-ga-un

laundry (process)	빨래	ppal-lae
washing machine	세탁기	se-tak-gi
to do the laundry	빨래하다	ppal-lae-ha-da
laundry detergent	가루세제	ga-ru-se-je

73. Household appliances

TV set	텔레비전	tel-le-bi-jeon
tape recorder	카세트 플레이어	ka-se-teu peul-le-i-eo
VCR (video recorder)	비디오테이프 녹화기	bi-di-o-te-i-peu nok-wa-gi
radio	라디오	ra-di-o
player (CD, MP3, etc.)	플레이어	peul-le-i-eo

video projector	프로젝터	peu-ro-jek-teo
home movie theater	홈씨어터	hom-ssi-eo-teo
DVD player	디비디 플레이어	di-bi-di peul-le-i-eo
amplifier	앰프	aem-peu
video game console	게임기	ge-im-gi

video camera	캠코더	kaem-ko-deo
camera (photo)	카메라	ka-me-ra
digital camera	디지털 카메라	di-ji-teol ka-me-ra

vacuum cleaner	진공 청소기	jin-gong cheong-so-gi
iron (e.g., steam ~)	다리미	da-ri-mi
ironing board	다림질 판	da-rim-jil pan

| telephone | 전화 | jeon-hwa |
| cell phone | 휴대폰 | hyu-dae-pon |

typewriter	타자기	ta-ja-gi
sewing machine	재봉틀	jae-bong-teul
microphone	마이크	ma-i-keu
headphones	헤드폰	he-deu-pon
remote control (TV)	원격 조종	won-gyeok jo-jong
CD, compact disc	씨디	ssi-di
cassette, tape	테이프	te-i-peu
vinyl record	레코드 판	re-ko-deu pan

T&P BOOKS

THE EARTH. WEATHER

T&P Books Publishing

space	우주	u-ju
space (as adj)	우주의	u-ju-ui
outer space	우주 공간	u-ju gong-gan
world	세계	se-gye
universe	우주	u-ju
galaxy	은하	eun-ha
star	별, 항성	byeol, hang-seong
constellation	별자리	byeol-ja-ri
planet	행성	haeng-seong
satellite	인공위성	in-gong-wi-seong
meteorite	운석	un-seok
comet	혜성	hye-seong
asteroid	소행성	so-haeng-seong
orbit	궤도	gwe-do
to revolve	회전한다	hoe-jeon-han-da
(~ around the Earth)		
atmosphere	대기	dae-gi
the Sun	태양	tae-yang
solar system	태양계	tae-yang-gye
solar eclipse	일식	il-sik
the Earth	지구	ji-gu
the Moon	달	dal
Mars	화성	hwa-seong
Venus	금성	geum-seong
Jupiter	목성	mok-seong
Saturn	토성	to-seong
Mercury	수성	su-seong
Uranus	천왕성	cheon-wang-seong
Neptune	해왕성	hae-wang-seong
Pluto	명왕성	myeong-wang-seong
Milky Way	은하수	eun-ha-su
Great Bear (Ursa Major)	큰곰자리	keun-gom-ja-ri
North Star	북극성	buk-geuk-seong
Martian	화성인	hwa-seong-in
extraterrestrial (n)	외계인	oe-gye-in

alien	외계인	oe-gye-in
flying saucer	비행 접시	bi-haeng jeop-si
spaceship	우주선	u-ju-seon
space station	우주 정거장	u-ju jeong-nyu-jang
engine	엔진	en-jin
nozzle	노즐	no-jeul
fuel	연료	yeol-lyo
cockpit, flight deck	조종석	jo-jong-seok
antenna	안테나	an-te-na
porthole	현창	hyeon-chang
solar panel	태양 전지	tae-yang jeon-ji
spacesuit	우주복	u-ju-bok
weightlessness	무중력	mu-jung-nyeok
oxygen	산소	san-so
docking (in space)	도킹	do-king
to dock (vi, vt)	도킹하다	do-king-ha-da
observatory	천문대	cheon-mun-dae
telescope	망원경	mang-won-gyeong
to observe (vt)	관찰하다	gwan-chal-ha-da
to explore (vt)	탐험하다	tam-heom-ha-da

75. The Earth

the Earth	지구	ji-gu
the globe (the Earth)	지구	ji-gu
planet	행성	haeng-seong
atmosphere	대기	dae-gi
geography	지리학	ji-ri-hak
nature	자연	ja-yeon
globe (table ~)	지구의	ji-gu-ui
map	지도	ji-do
atlas	지도첩	ji-do-cheop
Europe	유럽	yu-reop
Asia	아시아	a-si-a
Africa	아프리카	a-peu-ri-ka
Australia	호주	ho-ju
America	아메리카 대륙	a-me-ri-ka dae-ryuk
North America	북아메리카	bu-ga-me-ri-ka
South America	남아메리카	nam-a-me-ri-ka
Antarctica	남극 대륙	nam-geuk dae-ryuk
the Arctic	극지방	geuk-ji-bang

76. Cardinal directions

north	북쪽	buk-jjok
to the north	북쪽으로	buk-jjo-geu-ro
in the north	북쪽에	buk-jjo-ge
northern (adj)	북쪽의	buk-jjo-gui

south	남쪽	nam-jjok
to the south	남쪽으로	nam-jjo-geu-ro
in the south	남쪽에	nam-jjo-ge
southern (adj)	남쪽의	nam-jjo-gui

west	서쪽	seo-jjok
to the west	서쪽으로	seo-jjo-geu-ro
in the west	서쪽에	seo-jjo-ge
western (adj)	서쪽의	seo-jjo-gui

east	동쪽	dong-jjok
to the east	동쪽으로	dong-jjo-geu-ro
in the east	동쪽에	dong-jjo-ge
eastern (adj)	동쪽의	dong-jjo-gui

77. Sea. Ocean

sea	바다	ba-da
ocean	대양	dae-yang
gulf (bay)	만	man
straits	해협	hae-hyeop

continent (mainland)	대륙	dae-ryuk
island	섬	seom
peninsula	반도	ban-do
archipelago	군도	gun-do

bay, cove	만	man
harbor	항구	hang-gu
lagoon	석호	seok-o
cape	곶	got

atoll	환초	hwan-cho
reef	암초	am-cho
coral	산호	san-ho
coral reef	산호초	san-ho-cho

deep (adj)	깊은	gi-peun
depth (deep water)	깊이	gi-pi
trench (e.g., Mariana ~)	해구	hae-gu
current (Ocean ~)	해류	hae-ryu
to surround (bathe)	둘러싸다	dul-leo-ssa-da

shore	해변	hae-byeon
coast	바닷가	ba-dat-ga
flow (flood tide)	밀물	mil-mul
ebb (ebb tide)	썰물	sseol-mul
shoal	모래톱	mo-rae-top
bottom (~ of the sea)	해저	hae-jeo
wave	파도	pa-do
crest (~ of a wave)	물마루	mul-ma-ru
spume (sea foam)	거품	geo-pum
hurricane	허리케인	heo-ri-ke-in
tsunami	해일	hae-il
calm (dead ~)	고요함	go-yo-ham
quiet, calm (adj)	고요한	go-yo-han
pole	극	geuk
polar (adj)	극지의	geuk-ji-ui
latitude	위도	wi-do
longitude	경도	gyeong-do
parallel	위도선	wi-do-seon
equator	적도	jeok-do
sky	하늘	ha-neul
horizon	수평선	su-pyeong-seon
air	공기	gong-gi
lighthouse	등대	deung-dae
to dive (vi)	뛰어들다	ttwi-eo-deul-da
to sink (ab. boat)	가라앉다	ga-ra-an-da
treasures	보물	bo-mul

78. Seas' and Oceans' names

Atlantic Ocean	대서양	dae-seo-yang
Indian Ocean	인도양	in-do-yang
Pacific Ocean	태평양	tae-pyeong-yang
Arctic Ocean	북극해	buk-geuk-ae
Black Sea	흑해	heuk-ae
Red Sea	홍해	hong-hae
Yellow Sea	황해	hwang-hae
White Sea	백해	baek-ae
Caspian Sea	카스피 해	ka-seu-pi hae
Dead Sea	사해	sa-hae
Mediterranean Sea	지중해	ji-jung-hae
Aegean Sea	에게 해	e-ge hae

Adriatic Sea	아드리아 해	a-deu-ri-a hae
Arabian Sea	아라비아 해	a-ra-bi-a hae
Sea of Japan	동해	dong-hae
Bering Sea	베링 해	be-ring hae
South China Sea	남중국해	nam-jung-guk-ae

Coral Sea	산호해	san-ho-hae
Tasman Sea	태즈먼 해	tae-jeu-meon hae
Caribbean Sea	카리브 해	ka-ri-beu hae

| Barents Sea | 바렌츠 해 | ba-ren-cheu hae |
| Kara Sea | 카라 해 | ka-ra hae |

North Sea	북해	buk-ae
Baltic Sea	발트 해	bal-teu hae
Norwegian Sea	노르웨이 해	no-reu-we-i hae

79. Mountains

mountain	산	san
mountain range	산맥	san-maek
mountain ridge	능선	neung-seon

summit, top	정상	jeong-sang
peak	봉우리	bong-u-ri
foot (~ of the mountain)	기슭	gi-seuk
slope (mountainside)	경사면	gyeong-sa-myeon

volcano	화산	hwa-san
active volcano	활화산	hwal-hwa-san
dormant volcano	사화산	sa-hwa-san

eruption	폭발	pok-bal
crater	분화구	bun-hwa-gu
magma	마그마	ma-geu-ma
lava	용암	yong-am
molten (~ lava)	녹은	no-geun

canyon	협곡	hyeop-gok
gorge	협곡	hyeop-gok
crevice	갈라진	gal-la-jin

pass, col	산길	san-gil
plateau	고원	go-won
cliff	절벽	jeol-byeok
hill	언덕, 작은 산	eon-deok, ja-geun san

glacier	빙하	bing-ha
waterfall	폭포	pok-po
geyser	간헐천	gan-heol-cheon

lake	호수	ho-su
plain	평원	pyeong-won
landscape	경관	gyeong-gwan
echo	메아리	me-a-ri

alpinist	등산가	deung-san-ga
rock climber	암벽 등반가	am-byeok deung-ban-ga
to conquer (in climbing)	정복하다	jeong-bok-a-da
climb (an easy ~)	등반	deung-ban

80. Mountains names

The Alps	알프스 산맥	al-peu-seu san-maek
Mont Blanc	몽블랑 산	mong-beul-lang san
The Pyrenees	피레네 산맥	pi-re-ne san-maek

The Carpathians	카르파티아 산맥	ka-reu-pa-ti-a san-maek
The Ural Mountains	우랄 산맥	u-ral san-maek
The Caucasus Mountains	코카서스 산맥	ko-ka-seo-seu san-maek
Mount Elbrus	엘브루스 산	el-beu-ru-seu san

The Altai Mountains	알타이 산맥	al-ta-i san-maek
The Tian Shan	톈샨 산맥	ten-syan san-maek
The Pamir Mountains	파미르 고원	pa-mi-reu go-won
The Himalayas	히말라야 산맥	hi-mal-la-ya san-maek
Mount Everest	에베레스트 산	e-be-re-seu-teu san

| The Andes | 안데스 산맥 | an-de-seu san-maek |
| Mount Kilimanjaro | 킬리만자로 산 | kil-li-man-ja-ro san |

81. Rivers

river	강	gang
spring (natural source)	샘	saem
riverbed (river channel)	강바닥	gang-ba-dak
basin (river valley)	유역	yu-yeok
to flow into ...	… 로 흘러가다	… ro heul-leo-ga-da

| tributary | 지류 | ji-ryu |
| bank (of river) | 둑 | duk |

current (stream)	흐름	heu-reum
downstream (adv)	하류로	gang ha-ryu-ro
upstream (adv)	상류로	sang-nyu-ro

inundation	홍수	hong-su
flooding	홍수	hong-su
to overflow (vi)	범람하다	beom-nam-ha-da

to flood (vt)	범람하다	beom-nam-ha-da
shallow (shoal)	얕은 곳	ya-teun got
rapids	여울	yeo-ul
dam	댐	daem
canal	운하	un-ha
reservoir (artificial lake)	저수지	jeo-su-ji
sluice, lock	수문	su-mun
water body (pond, etc.)	저장 수량	jeo-jang su-ryang
swamp (marshland)	늪, 소택지	neup, so-taek-ji
bog, marsh	수렁	su-reong
whirlpool	소용돌이	so-yong-do-ri
stream (brook)	개울, 시내	gae-ul, si-nae
drinking (ab. water)	마실 수 있는	ma-sil su in-neun
fresh (~ water)	민물의	min-mu-rui
ice	얼음	eo-reum
to freeze over (ab. river, etc.)	얼다	eol-da

82. Rivers' names

Seine	센 강	sen gang
Loire	루아르 강	ru-a-reu gang
Thames	템스 강	tem-seu gang
Rhine	라인 강	ra-in gang
Danube	도나우 강	do-na-u gang
Volga	볼가 강	bol-ga gang
Don	돈 강	don gang
Lena	레나 강	re-na gang
Yellow River	황허강	hwang-heo-gang
Yangtze	양자강	yang-ja-gang
Mekong	메콩 강	me-kong gang
Ganges	갠지스 강	gaen-ji-seu gang
Nile River	나일 강	na-il gang
Congo River	콩고 강	kong-go gang
Okavango River	오카방고 강	o-ka-bang-go gang
Zambezi River	잠베지 강	jam-be-ji gang
Limpopo River	림포포 강	rim-po-po gang

83. Forest

forest, wood	숲	sup
forest (as adj)	산림의	sal-li-mui

thick forest	밀림	mil-lim
grove	작은 숲	ja-geun sup
forest clearing	빈터	bin-teo
thicket	덤불	deom-bul
scrubland	관목지	gwan-mok-ji
footpath (troddenpath)	오솔길	o-sol-gil
gully	도랑	do-rang
tree	나무	na-mu
leaf	잎	ip
leaves (foliage)	나뭇잎	na-mun-nip
fall of leaves	낙엽	na-gyeop
to fall (ab. leaves)	떨어지다	tteo-reo-ji-da
branch	가지	ga-ji
bough	큰 가지	keun ga-ji
bud (on shrub, tree)	잎눈	im-nun
needle (of pine tree)	바늘	ba-neul
pine cone	솔방울	sol-bang-ul
hollow (in a tree)	구멍	gu-meong
nest	둥지	dung-ji
burrow (animal hole)	굴	gul
trunk	몸통	mom-tong
root	뿌리	ppu-ri
bark	겁질	kkeop-jil
moss	이끼	i-kki
to uproot (remove trees or tree stumps)	수목을 통제 뽑다	su-mo-geul tong-jjae ppop-da
to chop down	자르다	ja-reu-da
to deforest (vt)	삼림을 없애다	sam-ni-meul reop-sae-da
tree stump	그루터기	geu-ru-teo-gi
campfire	모닥불	mo-dak-bul
forest fire	산불	san-bul
to extinguish (vt)	끄다	kkeu-da
forest ranger	산림경비원	sal-lim-gyeong-bi-won
protection	보호	bo-ho
to protect (~ nature)	보호하다	bo-ho-ha-da
poacher	밀렵자	mil-lyeop-ja
steel trap	덫	deot
to gather, to pick (vt)	따다	tta-da
to lose one's way	길을 잃다	gi-reul ril-ta

84. Natural resources

natural resources	천연 자원	cheo-nyeon ja-won
deposits	매장량	mae-jang-nyang
field (e.g., oilfield)	지역	ji-yeok
to mine (extract)	채광하다	chae-gwang-ha-da
mining (extraction)	막장일	mak-jang-il
ore	광석	gwang-seok
mine (e.g., for coal)	광산	gwang-san
shaft (mine ~)	갱도	gaeng-do
miner	광부	gwang-bu
gas (natural ~)	가스	ga-seu
gas pipeline	가스관	ga-seu-gwan
oil (petroleum)	석유	seo-gyu
oil pipeline	석유 파이프라인	seo-gyu pa-i-peu-ra-in
oil well	유정	yu-jeong
derrick (tower)	유정탑	yu-jeong-tap
tanker	유조선	yu-jo-seon
sand	모래	mo-rae
limestone	석회석	seok-oe-seok
gravel	자갈	ja-gal
peat	토탄	to-tan
clay	점토	jeom-to
coal	석탄	seok-tan
iron (ore)	철	cheol
gold	금	geum
silver	은	eun
nickel	니켈	ni-kel
copper	구리	gu-ri
zinc	아연	a-yeon
manganese	망간	mang-gan
mercury	수은	su-eun
lead	납	nap
mineral	광물	gwang-mul
crystal	수정	su-jeong
marble	대리석	dae-ri-seok
uranium	우라늄	u-ra-nyum

85. Weather

weather	날씨	nal-ssi
weather forecast	일기 예보	il-gi ye-bo

temperature	온도	on-do
thermometer	온도계	on-do-gye
barometer	기압계	gi-ap-gye

humidity	습함, 습기	seu-pam, seup-gi
heat (extreme ~)	더위	deo-wi
hot (torrid)	더운	deo-un
it's hot	덥다	deop-da

| it's warm | 따뜻하다 | tta-tteu-ta-da |
| warm (moderately hot) | 따뜻한 | tta-tteu-tan |

| it's cold | 춥다 | chup-da |
| cold (adj) | 추운 | chu-un |

sun	해	hae
to shine (vi)	빛나다	bin-na-da
sunny (day)	화창한	hwa-chang-han
to come up (vi)	뜨다	tteu-da
to set (vi)	지다	ji-da

cloud	구름	gu-reum
cloudy (adj)	구름의	gu-reum-ui
somber (gloomy)	흐린	heu-rin

rain	비	bi
it's raining	비가 오다	bi-ga o-da
rainy (~ day, weather)	비가 오는	bi-ga o-neun
to drizzle (vi)	이슬비가 내리다	i-seul-bi-ga nae-ri-da

pouring rain	억수	eok-su
downpour	호우	ho-u
heavy (e.g., ~ rain)	심한	sim-han
puddle	웅덩이	ung-deong-i
to get wet (in rain)	젖다	jeot-da

fog (mist)	안개	an-gae
foggy	안개가 자욱한	an-gae-ga ja-uk-an
snow	눈	nun
it's snowing	눈이 오다	nun-i o-da

86. Severe weather. Natural disasters

thunderstorm	뇌우	noe-u
lightning (~ strike)	번개	beon-gae
to flash (vi)	번쩍이다	beon-jjeo-gi-da

thunder	천둥	cheon-dung
to thunder (vi)	천둥이 치다	cheon-dung-i chi-da
it's thundering	천둥이 치다	cheon-dung-i chi-da

hail	싸락눈	ssa-rang-nun
it's hailing	싸락눈이 내리다	ssa-rang-nun-i nae-ri-da
to flood (vt)	범람하다	beom-nam-ha-da
flood, inundation	홍수	hong-su
earthquake	지진	ji-jin
tremor, quake	진동	jin-dong
epicenter	진앙	jin-ang
eruption	폭발	pok-bal
lava	용암	yong-am
twister	회오리바람	hoe-o-ri-ba-ram
tornado	토네이도	to-ne-i-do
typhoon	태풍	tae-pung
hurricane	허리케인	heo-ri-ke-in
storm	폭풍우	pok-pung-u
tsunami	해일	hae-il
fire (accident)	불	bul
disaster	재해	jae-hae
meteorite	운석	un-seok
avalanche	눈사태	nun-sa-tae
snowslide	눈사태	nun-sa-tae
blizzard	눈보라	nun-bo-ra
snowstorm	눈보라	nun-bo-ra

FAUNA

T&P Books Publishing

predator	육식 동물	yuk-sik dong-mul
tiger	호랑이	ho-rang-i
lion	사자	sa-ja
wolf	이리	i-ri
fox	여우	yeo-u
jaguar	재규어	jae-gyu-eo
leopard	표범	pyo-beom
cheetah	치타	chi-ta
puma	퓨마	pyu-ma
snow leopard	눈표범	nun-pyo-beom
lynx	스라소니	seu-ra-so-ni
coyote	코요테	ko-yo-te
jackal	재칼	jae-kal
hyena	하이에나	ha-i-e-na

88. Wild animals

animal	동물	dong-mul
beast (animal)	짐승	jim-seung
squirrel	다람쥐	da-ram-jwi
hedgehog	고슴도치	go-seum-do-chi
hare	토끼	to-kki
rabbit	굴토끼	gul-to-kki
badger	오소리	o-so-ri
raccoon	너구리	neo-gu-ri
hamster	햄스터	haem-seu-teo
marmot	마멋	ma-meot
mole	두더지	du-deo-ji
mouse	생쥐	saeng-jwi
rat	시궁쥐	si-gung-jwi
bat	박쥐	bak-jwi
ermine	북방족제비	buk-bang-jok-je-bi
sable	검은담비	geo-meun-dam-bi
marten	담비	dam-bi
mink	밍크	ming-keu

beaver	비버	bi-beo
otter	수달	su-dal
horse	말	mal
moose	엘크, 무스	el-keu, mu-seu
deer	사슴	sa-seum
camel	낙타	nak-ta
bison	미국들소	mi-guk-deul-so
aurochs	유럽들소	yu-reop-deul-so
buffalo	물소	mul-so
zebra	얼룩말	eol-lung-mal
antelope	영양	yeong-yang
roe deer	노루	no-ru
fallow deer	다마사슴	da-ma-sa-seum
chamois	샤모아	sya-mo-a
wild boar	멧돼지	met-dwae-ji
whale	고래	go-rae
seal	바다표범	ba-da-pyo-beom
walrus	바다코끼리	ba-da-ko-kki-ri
fur seal	물개	mul-gae
dolphin	돌고래	dol-go-rae
bear	곰	gom
polar bear	북극곰	buk-geuk-gom
panda	판다	pan-da
monkey	원숭이	won-sung-i
chimpanzee	침팬지	chim-paen-ji
orangutan	오랑우탄	o-rang-u-tan
gorilla	고릴라	go-ril-la
macaque	마카크	ma-ka-keu
gibbon	긴팔원숭이	gin-pa-rwon-sung-i
elephant	코끼리	ko-kki-ri
rhinoceros	코뿔소	ko-ppul-so
giraffe	기린	gi-rin
hippopotamus	하마	ha-ma
kangaroo	캥거루	kaeng-geo-ru
koala (bear)	코알라	ko-al-la
mongoose	몽구스	mong-gu-seu
chinchilla	친칠라	chin-chil-la
skunk	스컹크	seu-keong-keu
porcupine	호저	ho-jeo

89. Domestic animals

cat	고양이	go-yang-i
tomcat	수고양이	su-go-yang-i
horse	말	mal
stallion (male horse)	수말, 종마	su-mal, jong-ma
mare	암말	am-mal
cow	암소	am-so
bull	황소	hwang-so
ox	수소	su-so
sheep (ewe)	양, 암양	yang, a-myang
ram	수양	su-yang
goat	염소	yeom-so
billy goat, he-goat	숫염소	sun-nyeom-so
donkey	당나귀	dang-na-gwi
mule	노새	no-sae
pig, hog	돼지	dwae-ji
piglet	돼지 새끼	dwae-ji sae-kki
rabbit	집토끼	jip-to-kki
hen (chicken)	암탉	am-tak
rooster	수탉	su-tak
duck	집오리	ji-bo-ri
drake	수오리	su-o-ri
goose	집거위	jip-geo-wi
tom turkey, gobbler	수칠면조	su-chil-myeon-jo
turkey (hen)	칠면조	chil-myeon-jo
domestic animals	가축	ga-chuk
tame (e.g., ~ hamster)	길들여진	gil-deu-ryeo-jin
to tame (vt)	길들이다	gil-deu-ri-da
to breed (vt)	사육하다, 기르다	sa-yuk-a-da, gi-reu-da
farm	농장	nong-jang
poultry	가금	ga-geum
cattle	가축	ga-chuk
herd (cattle)	떼	tte
stable	마구간	ma-gu-gan
pigpen	돼지 우리	dwae-ji u-ri
cowshed	외양간	oe-yang-gan
rabbit hutch	토끼장	to-kki-jang
hen house	닭장	dak-jang

90. Birds

bird	새	sae
pigeon	비둘기	bi-dul-gi
sparrow	참새	cham-sae
tit (great tit)	박새	bak-sae
magpie	까치	kka-chi
raven	갈가마귀	gal-ga-ma-gwi
crow	까마귀	kka-ma-gwi
jackdaw	갈가마귀	gal-ga-ma-gwi
rook	떼까마귀	ttae-kka-ma-gwi
duck	오리	o-ri
goose	거위	geo-wi
pheasant	꿩	kkwong
eagle	독수리	dok-su-ri
hawk	매	mae
falcon	매	mae
vulture	독수리, 콘도르	dok-su-ri, kon-do-reu
condor (Andean ~)	콘도르	kon-do-reu
swan	백조	baek-jo
crane	두루미	du-ru-mi
stork	황새	hwang-sae
parrot	앵무새	aeng-mu-sae
hummingbird	벌새	beol-sae
peacock	공작	gong-jak
ostrich	타조	ta-jo
heron	왜가리	wae-ga-ri
flamingo	플라밍고	peul-la-ming-go
pelican	펠리컨	pel-li-keon
nightingale	나이팅게일	na-i-ting-ge-il
swallow	제비	je-bi
thrush	지빠귀	ji-ppa-gwi
song thrush	노래지빠귀	no-rae-ji-ppa-gwi
blackbird	대륙검은지빠귀	dae-ryuk-geo-meun-ji-ppa-gwi
swift	칼새	kal-sae
lark	종다리	jong-da-ri
quail	메추라기	me-chu-ra-gi
woodpecker	딱따구리	ttak-tta-gu-ri
cuckoo	뻐꾸기	ppeo-kku-gi
owl	올빼미	ol-ppae-mi

eagle owl	수리부엉이	su-ri-bu-eong-i
wood grouse	큰뇌조	keun-noe-jo
black grouse	멧닭	met-dak
partridge	자고	ja-go

starling	찌르레기	jji-reu-re-gi
canary	카나리아	ka-na-ri-a
chaffinch	되새	doe-sae
bullfinch	피리새	pi-ri-sae

seagull	갈매기	gal-mae-gi
albatross	신천옹	sin-cheon-ong
penguin	펭귄	peng-gwin

91. Fish. Marine animals

bream	도미류	do-mi-ryu
carp	잉어	ing-eo
perch	농어의 일종	nong-eo-ui il-jong
catfish	메기	me-gi
pike	북부민물꼬치고기	buk-bu-min-mul-kko-chi-go-gi

| salmon | 연어 | yeon-eo |
| sturgeon | 철갑상어 | cheol-gap-sang-eo |

herring	청어	cheong-eo
Atlantic salmon	대서양 연어	dae-seo-yang yeon-eo
mackerel	고등어	go-deung-eo
flatfish	넙치	neop-chi

cod	대구	dae-gu
tuna	참치	cham-chi
trout	송어	song-eo

eel	뱀장어	baem-jang-eo
electric ray	시끈가오리	si-kkeun-ga-o-ri
moray eel	곰치	gom-chi
piranha	피라니아	pi-ra-ni-a

shark	상어	sang-eo
dolphin	돌고래	dol-go-rae
whale	고래	go-rae

crab	게	ge
jellyfish	해파리	hae-pa-ri
octopus	낙지	nak-ji

| starfish | 불가사리 | bul-ga-sa-ri |
| sea urchin | 성게 | seong-ge |

seahorse	해마	hae-ma
oyster	굴	gul
shrimp	새우	sae-u
lobster	바닷가재	ba-dat-ga-jae
spiny lobster	대하	dae-ha

92. Amphibians. Reptiles

snake	뱀	baem
venomous (snake)	독이 있는	do-gi in-neun
viper	살무사	sal-mu-sa
cobra	코브라	ko-beu-ra
python	비단뱀	bi-dan-baem
boa	보아	bo-a
grass snake	풀뱀	pul-baem
rattle snake	방울뱀	bang-ul-baem
anaconda	아나콘다	a-na-kon-da
lizard	도마뱀	do-ma-baem
iguana	이구아나	i-gu-a-na
salamander	도롱뇽	do-rong-nyong
chameleon	카멜레온	ka-mel-le-on
scorpion	전갈	jeon-gal
turtle	거북	geo-buk
frog	개구리	gae-gu-ri
toad	두꺼비	du-kkeo-bi
crocodile	악어	a-geo

93. Insects

insect, bug	곤충	gon-chung
butterfly	나비	na-bi
ant	개미	gae-mi
fly	파리	pa-ri
mosquito	모기	mo-gi
beetle	딱정벌레	ttak-jeong-beol-le
wasp	말벌	mal-beol
bee	꿀벌	kkul-beol
bumblebee	호박벌	ho-bak-beol
gadfly (botfly)	쇠파리	soe-pa-ri
spider	거미	geo-mi
spiderweb	거미줄	geo-mi-jul
dragonfly	잠자리	jam-ja-ri

grasshopper	메뚜기	me-ttu-gi
moth (night butterfly)	나방	na-bang
cockroach	바퀴벌레	ba-kwi-beol-le
tick	진드기	jin-deu-gi
flea	벼룩	byeo-ruk
midge	깔따구	kkal-tta-gu
locust	메뚜기	me-ttu-gi
snail	달팽이	dal-paeng-i
cricket	귀뚜라미	gwi-ttu-ra-mi
lightning bug	개똥벌레	gae-ttong-beol-le
ladybug	무당벌레	mu-dang-beol-le
cockchafer	왕풍뎅이	wang-pung-deng-i
leech	거머리	geo-meo-ri
caterpillar	애벌레	ae-beol-le
earthworm	지렁이	ji-reong-i
larva	애벌레	ae-beol-le

FLORA

T&P Books Publishing

tree	나무	na-mu
deciduous (adj)	낙엽수의	na-gyeop-su-ui
coniferous (adj)	침엽수의	chi-myeop-su-ui
evergreen (adj)	상록의	sang-no-gui
apple tree	사과나무	sa-gwa-na-mu
pear tree	배나무	bae-na-mu
cherry tree	벚나무	beon-na-mu
plum tree	자두나무	ja-du-na-mu
birch	자작나무	ja-jang-na-mu
oak	오크	o-keu
linden tree	보리수	bo-ri-su
aspen	사시나무	sa-si-na-mu
maple	단풍나무	dan-pung-na-mu
spruce	가문비나무	ga-mun-bi-na-mu
pine	소나무	so-na-mu
larch	낙엽송	na-gyeop-song
fir tree	전나무	jeon-na-mu
cedar	시다	si-da
poplar	포플러	po-peul-leo
rowan	마가목	ma-ga-mok
willow	버드나무	beo-deu-na-mu
alder	오리나무	o-ri-na-mu
beech	너도밤나무	neo-do-bam-na-mu
elm	느릅나무	neu-reum-na-mu
ash (tree)	물푸레나무	mul-pu-re-na-mu
chestnut	밤나무	bam-na-mu
magnolia	목련	mong-nyeon
palm tree	야자나무	ya-ja-na-mu
cypress	사이프러스	sa-i-peu-reo-seu
mangrove	맹그로브	maeng-geu-ro-beu
baobab	바오밤나무	ba-o-bam-na-mu
eucalyptus	유칼립투스	yu-kal-lip-tu-seu
sequoia	세쿼이아	se-kwo-i-a

95. Shrubs

bush	덤불	deom-bul
shrub	관목	gwan-mok
grapevine	포도 덩굴	po-do deong-gul
vineyard	포도밭	po-do-bat
raspberry bush	라즈베리	ra-jeu-be-ri
redcurrant bush	레드커런트 나무	re-deu-keo-reon-teu na-mu
gooseberry bush	구스베리 나무	gu-seu-be-ri na-mu
acacia	아카시아	a-ka-si-a
barberry	매자나무	mae-ja-na-mu
jasmine	재스민	jae-seu-min
juniper	두송	du-song
rosebush	장미 덤불	jang-mi deom-bul
dog rose	찔레나무	jjil-le-na-mu

96. Fruits. Berries

apple	사과	sa-gwa
pear	배	bae
plum	자두	ja-du
strawberry (garden ~)	딸기	ttal-gi
sour cherry	신양	si-nyang
sweet cherry	양벚나무	yang-beon-na-mu
grape	포도	po-do
raspberry	라즈베리	ra-jeu-be-ri
blackcurrant	블랙커런트	beul-laek-keo-ren-teu
redcurrant	레드커런트	re-deu-keo-ren-teu
gooseberry	구스베리	gu-seu-be-ri
cranberry	크랜베리	keu-raen-be-ri
orange	오렌지	o-ren-ji
mandarin	귤	gyul
pineapple	파인애플	pa-in-ae-peul
banana	바나나	ba-na-na
date	대추야자	dae-chu-ya-ja
lemon	레몬	re-mon
apricot	살구	sal-gu
peach	복숭아	bok-sung-a
kiwi	키위	ki-wi
grapefruit	자몽	ja-mong

berry	장과	jang-gwa
berries	장과류	jang-gwa-ryu
cowberry	월귤나무	wol-gyul-la-mu
wild strawberry	야생딸기	ya-saeng-ttal-gi
bilberry	빌베리	bil-be-ri

97. Flowers. Plants

| flower | 꽃 | kkot |
| bouquet (of flowers) | 꽃다발 | kkot-da-bal |

rose (flower)	장미	jang-mi
tulip	튤립	tyul-lip
carnation	카네이션	ka-ne-i-syeon
gladiolus	글라디올러스	geul-la-di-ol-leo-seu

cornflower	수레국화	su-re-guk-wa
harebell	실잔대	sil-jan-dae
dandelion	민들레	min-deul-le
camomile	캐모마일	kae-mo-ma-il

aloe	알로에	al-lo-e
cactus	선인장	seon-in-jang
rubber plant, ficus	고무나무	go-mu-na-mu

lily	백합	baek-ap
geranium	제라늄	je-ra-nyum
hyacinth	히아신스	hi-a-sin-seu

mimosa	미모사	mi-mo-sa
narcissus	수선화	su-seon-hwa
nasturtium	한련	hal-lyeon

orchid	난초	nan-cho
peony	모란	mo-ran
violet	바이올렛	ba-i-ol-let

pansy	팬지	paen-ji
forget-me-not	물망초	mul-mang-cho
daisy	데이지	de-i-ji

poppy	양귀비	yang-gwi-bi
hemp	삼	sam
mint	박하	bak-a

| lily of the valley | 은방울꽃 | eun-bang-ul-kkot |
| snowdrop | 스노드롭 | seu-no-deu-rop |

| nettle | 쐐기풀 | sswae-gi-pul |
| sorrel | 수영 | su-yeong |

water lily	수련	su-ryeon
fern	고사리	go-sa-ri
lichen	이끼	i-kki

greenhouse (tropical ~)	온실	on-sil
lawn	잔디	jan-di
flowerbed	꽃밭	kkot-bat

plant	식물	sing-mul
grass	풀	pul
blade of grass	풀잎	pu-rip

leaf	잎	ip
petal	꽃잎	kko-chip
stem	줄기	jul-gi
tuber	구근	gu-geun

| young plant (shoot) | 새싹 | sae-ssak |
| thorn | 가시 | ga-si |

to blossom (vi)	피우다	pi-u-da
to fade, to wither	시들다	si-deul-da
smell (odor)	향기	hyang-gi
to cut (flowers)	자르다	ja-reu-da
to pick (a flower)	따다	tta-da

98. Cereals, grains

grain	곡물	gong-mul
cereal crops	곡류	gong-nyu
ear (of barley, etc.)	이삭	i-sak

wheat	밀	mil
rye	호밀	ho-mil
oats	귀리	gwi-ri
millet	수수, 기장	su-su, gi-jang
barley	보리	bo-ri

corn	옥수수	ok-su-su
rice	쌀	ssal
buckwheat	메밀	me-mil

pea plant	완두	wan-du
kidney bean	강낭콩	gang-nang-kong
soy	콩	kong
lentil	렌즈콩	ren-jeu-kong
beans (pulse crops)	콩	kong

T&P BOOKS

COUNTRIES OF
THE WORLD

T&P Books Publishing

Afghanistan	아프가니스탄	a-peu-ga-ni-seu-tan
Albania	알바니아	al-ba-ni-a
Argentina	아르헨티나	a-reu-hen-ti-na
Armenia	아르메니아	a-reu-me-ni-a
Australia	호주	ho-ju
Austria	오스트리아	o-seu-teu-ri-a
Azerbaijan	아제르바이잔	a-je-reu-ba-i-jan
The Bahamas	바하마	ba-ha-ma
Bangladesh	방글라데시	bang-geul-la-de-si
Belarus	벨로루시	bel-lo-ru-si
Belgium	벨기에	bel-gi-e
Bolivia	볼리비아	bol-li-bi-a
Bosnia and Herzegovina	보스니아 헤르체코비나	bo-seu-ni-a he-reu-che-ko-bi-na
Brazil	브라질	beu-ra-jil
Bulgaria	불가리아	bul-ga-ri-a
Cambodia	캄보디아	kam-bo-di-a
Canada	캐나다	kae-na-da
Chile	칠레	chil-le
China	중국	jung-guk
Colombia	콜롬비아	kol-lom-bi-a
Croatia	크로아티아	keu-ro-a-ti-a
Cuba	쿠바	ku-ba
Cyprus	키프로스	ki-peu-ro-seu
Czech Republic	체코	che-ko
Denmark	덴마크	den-ma-keu
Dominican Republic	도미니카 공화국	do-mi-ni-ka gong-hwa-guk
Ecuador	에콰도르	e-kwa-do-reu
Egypt	이집트	i-jip-teu
England	잉글랜드	ing-geul-laen-deu
Estonia	에스토니아	e-seu-to-ni-a
Finland	핀란드	pil-lan-deu
France	프랑스	peu-rang-seu
French Polynesia	폴리네시아	pol-li-ne-si-a
Georgia	그루지야	geu-ru-ji-ya
Germany	독일	do-gil
Ghana	가나	ga-na
Great Britain	영국	yeong-guk
Greece	그리스	geu-ri-seu
Haiti	아이티	a-i-ti
Hungary	헝가리	heong-ga-ri

100. Countries. Part 2

Iceland	아이슬란드	a-i-seul-lan-deu
India	인도	in-do
Indonesia	인도네시아	in-do-ne-si-a
Iran	이란	i-ran
Iraq	이라크	i-ra-keu
Ireland	아일랜드	a-il-laen-deu
Israel	이스라엘	i-seu-ra-el
Italy	이탈리아	i-tal-li-a
Jamaica	자메이카	ja-me-i-ka
Japan	일본	il-bon
Jordan	요르단	yo-reu-dan
Kazakhstan	카자흐스탄	ka-ja-heu-seu-tan
Kenya	케냐	ke-nya
Kirghizia	키르기스스탄	ki-reu-gi-seu-seu-tan
Kuwait	쿠웨이트	ku-we-i-teu
Laos	라오스	ra-o-seu
Latvia	라트비아	ra-teu-bi-a
Lebanon	레바논	re-ba-non
Libya	리비아	ri-bi-a
Liechtenstein	리히텐슈타인	ri-hi-ten-syu-ta-in
Lithuania	리투아니아	ri-tu-a-ni-a
Luxembourg	룩셈부르크	ruk-sem-bu-reu-keu
Macedonia (Republic of ~)	마케도니아	ma-ke-do-ni-a
Madagascar	마다가스카르	ma-da-ga-seu-ka-reu
Malaysia	말레이시아	mal-le-i-si-a
Malta	몰타	mol-ta
Mexico	멕시코	mek-si-ko
Moldova, Moldavia	몰도바	mol-do-ba
Monaco	모나코	mo-na-ko
Mongolia	몽골	mong-gol
Montenegro	몬테네그로	mon-te-ne-geu-ro
Morocco	모로코	mo-ro-ko
Myanmar	미얀마	mi-yan-ma
Namibia	나미비아	na-mi-bi-a
Nepal	네팔	ne-pal
Netherlands	네덜란드	ne-deol-lan-deu
New Zealand	뉴질랜드	nyu-jil-laen-deu
North Korea	북한	buk-an
Norway	노르웨이	no-reu-we-i

101. Countries. Part 3

Pakistan	파키스탄	pa-ki-seu-tan
Palestine	팔레스타인	pal-le-seu-ta-in

Panama	파나마	pa-na-ma
Paraguay	파라과이	pa-ra-gwa-i
Peru	페루	pe-ru
Poland	폴란드	pol-lan-deu
Portugal	포르투갈	po-reu-tu-gal
Romania	루마니아	ru-ma-ni-a
Russia	러시아	reo-si-a
Saudi Arabia	사우디아라비아	sa-u-di-a-ra-bi-a
Scotland	스코틀랜드	seu-ko-teul-laen-deu
Senegal	세네갈	se-ne-gal
Serbia	세르비아	se-reu-bi-a
Slovakia	슬로바키아	seul-lo-ba-ki-a
Slovenia	슬로베니아	seul-lo-be-ni-a
South Africa	남아프리카 공화국	nam-a-peu-ri-ka gong-hwa-guk
South Korea	한국	han-guk
Spain	스페인	seu-pe-in
Suriname	수리남	su-ri-nam
Sweden	스웨덴	seu-we-den
Switzerland	스위스	seu-wi-seu
Syria	시리아	si-ri-a
Taiwan	대만	dae-man
Tajikistan	타지키스탄	ta-ji-ki-seu-tan
Tanzania	탄자니아	tan-ja-ni-a
Tasmania	태즈메이니아	tae-jeu-me-i-ni-a
Thailand	태국	tae-guk
Tunisia	튀니지	twi-ni-ji
Turkey	터키	teo-ki
Turkmenistan	투르크메니스탄	tu-reu-keu-me-ni-seu-tan
Ukraine	우크라이나	u-keu-ra-i-na
United Arab Emirates	아랍에미리트	a-ra-be-mi-ri-teu
United States of America	미국	mi-guk
Uruguay	우루과이	u-ru-gwa-i
Uzbekistan	우즈베키스탄	u-jeu-be-ki-seu-tan
Vatican	바티칸	ba-ti-kan
Venezuela	베네수엘라	be-ne-su-el-la
Vietnam	베트남	be-teu-nam
Zanzibar	잔지바르	jan-ji-ba-reu

GASTRONOMIC GLOSSARY

This section contains a lot of words and terms associated with food. This dictionary will make it easier for you to understand the menu at a restaurant and choose the right dish

T&P Books Publishing

aftertaste	뒷 맛	dwit mat
almond	아몬드	a-mon-deu
anise	아니스	a-ni-seu
aperitif	아페리티프	a-pe-ri-ti-peu
appetite	식욕	si-gyok
appetizer	애피타이저	ae-pi-ta-i-jeo
apple	사과	sa-gwa
apricot	살구	sal-gu
artichoke	아티초크	a-ti-cho-keu
asparagus	아스파라거스	a-seu-pa-ra-geo-seu
Atlantic salmon	대서양 연어	dae-seo-yang yeon-eo
avocado	아보카도	a-bo-ka-do
bacon	베이컨	be-i-keon
banana	바나나	ba-na-na
barley	보리	bo-ri
bartender	바텐더	ba-ten-deo
basil	바질	ba-jil
bay leaf	월계수잎	wol-gye-su-ip
beans	콩	kong
beef	소고기	so-go-gi
beer	맥주	maek-ju
beetroot	비트	bi-teu
bell pepper	피망	pi-mang
berries	장과류	jang-gwa-ryu
berry	장과	jang-gwa
bilberry	빌베리	bil-be-ri
birch bolete	거친껠껠이그물버섯	geo-chin-kkeol-kkeo-ri-geu-mul-beo-seot
bitter	쓴	sseun
black coffee	블랙 커피	beul-laek keo-pi
black pepper	후추	hu-chu
black tea	홍차	hong-cha
blackberry	블랙베리	beul-laek-be-ri
blackcurrant	블랙커렌트	beul-laek-keo-ren-teu
boiled	삶은	sal-meun
bottle opener	병따개	byeong-tta-gae
bread	빵	ppang
breakfast	아침식사	a-chim-sik-sa
bream	도미류	do-mi-ryu
broccoli	브로콜리	beu-ro-kol-li
Brussels sprouts	방울다다기 양배추	bang-ul-da-da-gi yang-bae-chu
buckwheat	메밀	me-mil
butter	버터	beo-teo

buttercream	버터크림	beo-teo-keu-rim
cabbage	양배추	yang-bae-chu
cake	케이크	ke-i-keu
cake	케이크	ke-i-keu
calorie	칼로리	kal-lo-ri
can opener	깡통 따개	kkang-tong tta-gae
candy	사탕	sa-tang
canned food	통조림	tong-jo-rim
cappuccino	카푸치노	ka-pu-chi-no
caraway	캐러웨이	kae-reo-we-i
carbohydrates	탄수화물	tan-su-hwa-mul
carbonated	탄산의	tan-sa-nui
carp	잉어	ing-eo
carrot	당근	dang-geun
catfish	메기	me-gi
cauliflower	컬리플라워	keol-li-peul-la-wo
caviar	캐비어	kae-bi-eo
celery	셀러리	sel-leo-ri
cereal crops	곡류	gong-nyu
cereal grains	곡물	gong-mul
champagne	샴페인	syam-pe-in
chanterelle	살구버섯	sal-gu-beo-seot
check	계산서	gye-san-seo
cheese	치즈	chi-jeu
chewing gum	껌	kkeom
chicken	닭고기	dak-go-gi
chocolate	초콜릿	cho-kol-lit
chocolate	초콜릿의	cho-kol-lis-ui
cinnamon	계피	gye-pi
clear soup	육수	yuk-su
cloves	정향	jeong-hyang
cocktail	칵테일	kak-te-il
coconut	코코넛	ko-ko-neot
cod	대구	dae-gu
coffee	커피	keo-pi
coffee with milk	밀크 커피	mil-keu keo-pi
cognac	코냑	ko-nyak
cold	차가운	cha-ga-un
condensed milk	연유	yeo-nyu
condiment	양념	yang-nyeom
confectionery	과자류	gwa-ja-ryu
cookies	쿠키	ku-ki
coriander	고수	go-su
corkscrew	코르크 마개 뽑이	ko-reu-keu ma-gae ppo-bi
corn	옥수수	ok-su-su
corn	옥수수	ok-su-su
cornflakes	콘플레이크	kon-peul-le-i-keu
course, dish	요리, 코스	yo-ri, ko-seu
cowberry	월귤나무	wol-gyul-la-mu
crab	게	ge
cranberry	크랜베리	keu-raen-be-ri
cream	크림	keu-rim

crumb	부스러기	bu-seu-reo-gi
cucumber	오이	o-i
cuisine	요리	yo-ri
cup	컵	keop
dark beer	흑맥주	heung-maek-ju
date	대추야자	dae-chu-ya-ja
death cap	알광대버섯	al-gwang-dae-beo-seot
dessert	디저트	di-jeo-teu
diet	다이어트	da-i-eo-teu
dill	딜	dil
dinner	저녁식사	jeo-nyeok-sik-sa
dried	말린	mal-lin
drinking water	음료수	eum-nyo-su
duck	오리고기	o-ri-go-gi
ear	이삭	i-sak
edible mushroom	식용 버섯	si-gyong beo-seot
eel	뱀장어	baem-jang-eo
egg	계란	gye-ran
egg white	흰자	huin-ja
egg yolk	노른자	no-reun-ja
eggplant	가지	ga-ji
eggs	계란	gye-ran
Enjoy your meal!	맛있게 드십시오!	man-nit-ge deu-sip-si-o!
fats	지방	ji-bang
fig	무화과	mu-hwa-gwa
filling	속	sok
fish	생선	saeng-seon
flatfish	넙치	neop-chi
flour	밀가루	mil-ga-ru
fly agaric	광대버섯	gwang-dae-beo-seot
food	음식	eum-sik
fork	포크	po-keu
freshly squeezed juice	생과일주스	saeng-gwa-il-ju-seu
fried	튀긴	twi-gin
fried eggs	계란후라이	gye-ran-hu-ra-i
frozen	얼린	eol-lin
fruit	과일	gwa-il
game	사냥감	sa-nyang-gam
gammon	개먼	gae-meon
garlic	마늘	ma-neul
gin	진	jin
ginger	생강	saeng-gang
glass	유리잔	yu-ri-jan
glass	와인글라스	wa-in-geul-la-seu
goose	거위고기	geo-wi-go-gi
gooseberry	구스베리	gu-seu-be-ri
grain	곡물	gong-mul
grape	포도	po-do
grapefruit	자몽	ja-mong
green tea	녹차	nok-cha
greens	녹황색 채소	nok-wang-saek chae-so
halibut	넙치	neop-chi

ham	햄	haem
hamburger	다진 고기	da-jin go-gi
hamburger	햄버거	haem-beo-geo
hazelnut	개암	gae-am
herring	청어	cheong-eo
honey	꿀	kkul
horseradish	고추냉이	go-chu-naeng-i
hot	뜨거운	tteu-geo-un
ice	얼음	eo-reum
ice-cream	아이스크림	a-i-seu-keu-rim
instant coffee	인스턴트 커피	in-seu-teon-teu keo-pi
jam	잼	jaem
jam	잼	jaem
juice	주스	ju-seu
kidney bean	강낭콩	gang-nang-kong
kiwi	키위	ki-wi
knife	나이프	na-i-peu
lamb	양고기	yang-go-gi
lemon	레몬	re-mon
lemonade	레모네이드	re-mo-ne-i-deu
lentil	렌즈콩	ren-jeu-kong
lettuce	양상추	yang-sang-chu
light beer	라거	ra-geo
liqueur	리큐르	ri-kyu-reu
liquors	술	sul
liver	간	gan
lunch	점심식사	jeom-sim-sik-sa
mackerel	고등어	go-deung-eo
mandarin	귤	gyul
mango	망고	mang-go
margarine	마가린	ma-ga-rin
marmalade	마멀레이드	ma-meol-le-i-deu
mashed potatoes	으깬 감자	eu-kkaen gam-ja
mayonnaise	마요네즈	ma-yo-ne-jeu
meat	고기	go-gi
melon	멜론	mel-lon
menu	메뉴판	me-nyu-pan
milk	우유	u-yu
milkshake	밀크 셰이크	mil-keu sye-i-keu
millet	수수, 기장	su-su, gi-jang
mineral water	미네랄 워터	mi-ne-ral rwo-teo
morel	곰보버섯	gom-bo-beo-seot
mushroom	버섯	beo-seot
mustard	겨자	gyeo-ja
non-alcoholic	무알코올의	mu-al-ko-o-rui
noodles	면	myeon
oats	귀리	gwi-ri
olive oil	올리브유	ol-li-beu-yu
olives	올리브	ol-li-beu
omelet	오믈렛	o-meul-let
onion	양파	yang-pa
orange	오렌지	o-ren-ji

orange juice	오렌지 주스	o-ren-ji ju-seu
orange-cap boletus	등색껄껄이그물버섯	deung-saek-kkeol-kkeo-ri-geu-mul-beo-seot
oyster	굴	gul
pâté	파테	pa-te
papaya	파파야	pa-pa-ya
paprika	파프리카	pa-peu-ri-ka
parsley	파슬리	pa-seul-li
pasta	파스타	pa-seu-ta
pea	완두	wan-du
peach	복숭아	bok-sung-a
peanut	땅콩	ttang-kong
pear	배	bae
peel	껍질	kkeop-jil
perch	농어의 일종	nong-eo-ui il-jong
pickled	초절인	cho-jeo-rin
pie	파이	pa-i
piece	조각	jo-gak
pike	강꼬치고기	gang-kko-chi-go-gi
pineapple	파인애플	pa-in-ae-peul
pistachios	피스타치오	pi-seu-ta-chi-o
pizza	피자	pi-ja
plate	접시	jeop-si
plum	자두	ja-du
poisonous mushroom	독버섯	dok-beo-seot
pomegranate	석류	seong-nyu
pork	돼지고기	dwae-ji-go-gi
porridge	죽	juk
portion	분량	bul-lyang
potato	감자	gam-ja
proteins	단백질	dan-baek-jil
pub, bar	바	ba
pumpkin	호박	ho-bak
rabbit	토끼고기	to-kki-go-gi
radish	무	mu
raisin	건포도	geon-po-do
raspberry	라즈베리	ra-jeu-be-ri
recipe	요리법	yo-ri-beop
red pepper	고춧가루	go-chut-ga-ru
red wine	레드 와인	re-deu wa-in
redcurrant	레드커렌트	re-deu-keo-ren-teu
refreshing drink	청량 음료	cheong-nyang eum-nyo
rice	쌀	ssal
rum	럼	reom
russula	무당버섯	mu-dang-beo-seot
rye	호밀	ho-mil
saffron	사프란	sa-peu-ran
salad	샐러드	sael-leo-deu
salmon	연어	yeon-eo
salt	소금	so-geum
salty	짠	jjan
sandwich	샌드위치	saen-deu-wi-chi

sardine	정어리	jeong-eo-ri
sauce	소스	so-seu
saucer	받침 접시	bat-chim jeop-si
sausage	소시지	so-si-ji
seafood	해물	hae-mul
sesame	깨	kkae
shark	상어	sang-eo
shrimp	새우	sae-u
side dish	사이드 메뉴	sa-i-deu me-nyu
slice	조각	jo-gak
smoked	훈제된	hun-je-doen
soft drink	청량음료	cheong-nyang-eum-nyo
soup	수프	su-peu
soup spoon	숟가락	sut-ga-rak
sour cherry	신양	si-nyang
sour cream	사워크림	sa-wo-keu-rim
soy	콩	kong
spaghetti	스파게티	seu-pa-ge-ti
sparkling	탄산이 든	tan-san-i deun
spice	향료	hyang-nyo
spinach	시금치	si-geum-chi
spiny lobster	대하	dae-ha
spoon	숟가락	sut-ga-rak
squid	오징어	o-jing-eo
steak	비프스테이크	bi-peu-seu-te-i-keu
still	탄산 없는	tan-san neom-neun
strawberry	딸기	ttal-gi
sturgeon	철갑상어	cheol-gap-sang-eo
sugar	설탕	seol-tang
sunflower oil	해바라기유	hae-ba-ra-gi-yu
sweet	단	dan
sweet cherry	양벚나무	yang-beon-na-mu
taste, flavor	맛	mat
tasty	맛있는	man-nin-neun
tea	차	cha
teaspoon	티스푼	ti-seu-pun
tip	팁	tip
tomato	토마토	to-ma-to
tomato juice	토마토 주스	to-ma-to ju-seu
tongue	혀	hyeo
toothpick	이쑤시개	i-ssu-si-gae
trout	송어	song-eo
tuna	참치	cham-chi
turkey	칠면조고기	chil-myeon-jo-go-gi
turnip	순무	sun-mu
veal	송아지 고기	song-a-ji go-gi
vegetable oil	식물유	sing-mu-ryu
vegetables	채소	chae-so
vegetarian	채식주의자	chae-sik-ju-ui-ja
vegetarian	채식주의의	chae-sik-ju-ui-ui
vermouth	베르무트	be-reu-mu-teu
vienna sausage	비엔나 소시지	bi-en-na so-si-ji

vinegar	식초	sik-cho
vitamin	비타민	bi-ta-min
vodka	보드카	bo-deu-ka
waffles	와플	wa-peul
waiter	웨이터	we-i-teo
waitress	웨이트리스	we-i-teu-ri-seu
walnut	호두	ho-du
water	물	mul
watermelon	수박	su-bak
wheat	밀	mil
whiskey	위스키	wi-seu-ki
white wine	백 포도주	baek po-do-ju
wild strawberry	야생딸기	ya-saeng-ttal-gi
wine	와인	wa-in
wine list	와인 메뉴	wa-in me-nyu
with ice	얼음을 넣은	eo-reu-meul leo-eun
yogurt	요구르트	yo-gu-reu-teu
zucchini	애호박	ae-ho-bak

Korean-English gastronomic glossary

아보카도	a-bo-ka-do	avocado
아침식사	a-chim-sik-sa	breakfast
아이스크림	a-i-seu-keu-rim	ice-cream
아몬드	a-mon-deu	almond
아니스	a-ni-seu	anise
아페리티프	a-pe-ri-ti-peu	aperitif
아스파라거스	a-seu-pa-ra-geo-seu	asparagus
아티초크	a-ti-cho-keu	artichoke
애호박	ae-ho-bak	zucchini
애피타이저	ae-pi-ta-i-jeo	appetizer
알광대버섯	al-gwang-dae-beo-seot	death cap
바	ba	pub, bar
바질	ba-jil	basil
바나나	ba-na-na	banana
바텐더	ba-ten-deo	bartender
배	bae	pear
백 포도주	baek po-do-ju	white wine
뱀장어	baem-jang-eo	eel
방울다다기 양배추	bang-ul-da-da-gi yang-bae-chu	Brussels sprouts
받침 접시	bat-chim jeop-si	saucer
베이컨	be-i-keon	bacon
베르무트	be-reu-mu-teu	vermouth
버섯	beo-seot	mushroom
버터	beo-teo	butter
버터크림	beo-teo-keu-rim	buttercream
브로콜리	beu-ro-kol-li	broccoli
블랙 커피	beul-laek keo-pi	black coffee
블랙베리	beul-laek-be-ri	blackberry
블랙커렌트	beul-laek-keo-ren-teu	blackcurrant
비엔나 소시지	bi-en-na so-si-ji	vienna sausage
비프스테이크	bi-peu-seu-te-i-keu	steak
비타민	bi-ta-min	vitamin
비트	bi-teu	beetroot
빌베리	bil-be-ri	bilberry
보드카	bo-deu-ka	vodka
보리	bo-ri	barley
복숭아	bok-sung-a	peach
부스러기	bu-seu-reo-gi	crumb
분량	bul-lyang	portion
병따개	byeong-tta-gae	bottle opener
차	cha	tea
차가운	cha-ga-un	cold
채식주의자	chae-sik-ju-ui-ja	vegetarian

채식주의의	chae-sik-ju-ui-ui	vegetarian
채소	chae-so	vegetables
참치	cham-chi	tuna
철갑상어	cheol-gap-sang-eo	sturgeon
청어	cheong-eo	herring
청량 음료	cheong-nyang eum-nyo	refreshing drink
청량음료	cheong-nyang-eum-nyo	soft drink
치즈	chi-jeu	cheese
칠면조고기	chil-myeon-jo-go-gi	turkey
초절인	cho-jeo-rin	pickled
초콜릿의	cho-kol-lis-ui	chocolate
초콜릿	cho-kol-lit	chocolate
다이어트	da-i-eo-teu	diet
다진 고기	da-jin go-gi	hamburger
대추야자	dae-chu-ya-ja	date
대구	dae-gu	cod
대하	dae-ha	spiny lobster
대서양 연어	dae-seo-yang yeon-eo	Atlantic salmon
닭고기	dak-go-gi	chicken
단	dan	sweet
단백질	dan-baek-jil	proteins
당근	dang-geun	carrot
등색껠껠이그물버섯	deung-saek-kkeol-kkeo-ri-geu-mul-beo-seot	orange-cap boletus
디저트	di-jeo-teu	dessert
딜	dil	dill
도미류	do-mi-ryu	bream
독버섯	dok-beo-seot	poisonous mushroom
돼지고기	dwae-ji-go-gi	pork
뒷 맛	dwit mat	aftertaste
얼음을 넣은	eo-reu-meul leo-eun	with ice
얼음	eo-reum	ice
얼린	eol-lin	frozen
으깬 감자	eu-kkaen gam-ja	mashed potatoes
음료수	eum-nyo-su	drinking water
음식	eum-sik	food
가지	ga-ji	eggplant
개암	gae-am	hazelnut
개먼	gae-meon	gammon
감자	gam-ja	potato
간	gan	liver
강꼬치고기	gang-kko-chi-go-gi	pike
강낭콩	gang-nang-kong	kidney bean
게	ge	crab
거친껠껠이그물버섯	geo-chin-kkeol-kkeo-ri-geu-mul-beo-seot	birch bolete
거위고기	geo-wi-go-gi	goose
건포도	geon-po-do	raisin
고추냉이	go-chu-naeng-i	horseradish
고춧가루	go-chut-ga-ru	red pepper
고등어	go-deung-eo	mackerel
고기	go-gi	meat

고수	go-su	coriander
곰보버섯	gom-bo-beo-seot	morel
곡물	gong-mul	cereal grains
곡물	gong-mul	grain
곡류	gong-nyu	cereal crops
구스베리	gu-seu-be-ri	gooseberry
굴	gul	oyster
과일	gwa-il	fruit
과자류	gwa-ja-ryu	confectionery
광대버섯	gwang-dae-beo-seot	fly agaric
귀리	gwi-ri	oats
계피	gye-pi	cinnamon
계란	gye-ran	egg
계란	gye-ran	eggs
계란후라이	gye-ran-hu-ra-i	fried eggs
계산서	gye-san-seo	check
겨자	gyeo-ja	mustard
귤	gyul	mandarin
해바라기유	hae-ba-ra-gi-yu	sunflower oil
해물	hae-mul	seafood
햄	haem	ham
햄버거	haem-beo-geo	hamburger
흑맥주	heung-maek-ju	dark beer
호박	ho-bak	pumpkin
호두	ho-du	walnut
호밀	ho-mil	rye
홍차	hong-cha	black tea
후추	hu-chu	black pepper
흰자	huin-ja	egg white
훈제된	hun-je-doen	smoked
향료	hyang-nyo	spice
혀	hyeo	tongue
이삭	i-sak	ear
이쑤시개	i-ssu-si-gae	toothpick
인스턴트 커피	in-seu-teon-teu keo-pi	instant coffee
잉어	ing-eo	carp
자두	ja-du	plum
자몽	ja-mong	grapefruit
잼	jaem	jam
잼	jaem	jam
장과	jang-gwa	berry
장과류	jang-gwa-ryu	berries
저녁식사	jeo-nyeok-sik-sa	dinner
점심식사	jeom-sim-sik-sa	lunch
정어리	jeong-eo-ri	sardine
정향	jeong-hyang	cloves
접시	jeop-si	plate
지방	ji-bang	fats
진	jin	gin
짠	jjan	salty
조각	jo-gak	slice
조각	jo-gak	piece

주스	ju-seu	juice
죽	juk	porridge
카푸치노	ka-pu-chi-no	cappuccino
캐비어	kae-bi-eo	caviar
캐러웨이	kae-reo-we-i	caraway
칵테일	kak-te-il	cocktail
칼로리	kal-lo-ri	calorie
케이크	ke-i-keu	cake
케이크	ke-i-keu	cake
커피	keo-pi	coffee
컬리플라워	keol-li-peul-la-wo	cauliflower
컵	keop	cup
크랜베리	keu-raen-be-ri	cranberry
크림	keu-rim	cream
키위	ki-wi	kiwi
깨	kkae	sesame
깡통 따개	kkang-tong tta-gae	can opener
껌	kkeom	chewing gum
껍질	kkeop-jil	peel
꿀	kkul	honey
코코넛	ko-ko-neot	coconut
코냑	ko-nyak	cognac
코르크 마개 뽑이	ko-reu-keu ma-gae ppo-bi	corkscrew
콘플레이크	kon-peul-le-i-keu	cornflakes
콩	kong	beans
콩	kong	soy
쿠키	ku-ki	cookies
마가린	ma-ga-rin	margarine
마멀레이드	ma-meol-le-i-deu	marmalade
마늘	ma-neul	garlic
마요네즈	ma-yo-ne-jeu	mayonnaise
맥주	maek-ju	beer
말린	mal-lin	dried
맛있는	man-nin-neun	tasty
맛있게 드십시오!	man-nit-ge deu-sip-si-o!	Enjoy your meal!
망고	mang-go	mango
맛	mat	taste, flavor
메기	me-gi	catfish
메밀	me-mil	buckwheat
메뉴판	me-nyu-pan	menu
멜론	mel-lon	melon
미네랄 워터	mi-ne-ral rwo-teo	mineral water
밀	mil	wheat
밀가루	mil-ga-ru	flour
밀크 커피	mil-keu keo-pi	coffee with milk
밀크 셰이크	mil-keu sye-i-keu	milkshake
무	mu	radish
무알코올의	mu-al-ko-o-rui	non-alcoholic
무당버섯	mu-dang-beo-seot	russula
무화과	mu-hwa-gwa	fig
물	mul	water
면	myeon	noodles

나이프	na-i-peu	knife
넙치	neop-chi	halibut
넙치	neop-chi	flatfish
노른자	no-reun-ja	egg yolk
녹차	nok-cha	green tea
녹황색 채소	nok-wang-saek chae-so	greens
농어의 일종	nong-eo-ui il-jong	perch
오이	o-i	cucumber
오징어	o-jing-eo	squid
오믈렛	o-meul-let	omelet
오렌지	o-ren-ji	orange
오렌지 주스	o-ren-ji ju-seu	orange juice
오리고기	o-ri-go-gi	duck
옥수수	ok-su-su	corn
옥수수	ok-su-su	corn
올리브	ol-li-beu	olives
올리브유	ol-li-beu-yu	olive oil
파이	pa-i	pie
파인애플	pa-in-ae-peul	pineapple
파파야	pa-pa-ya	papaya
파프리카	pa-peu-ri-ka	paprika
파스타	pa-seu-ta	pasta
파슬리	pa-seul-li	parsley
파테	pa-te	pâté
피자	pi-ja	pizza
피망	pi-mang	bell pepper
피스타치오	pi-seu-ta-chi-o	pistachios
포도	po-do	grape
포크	po-keu	fork
빵	ppang	bread
라거	ra-geo	light beer
라즈베리	ra-jeu-be-ri	raspberry
레드 와인	re-deu wa-in	red wine
레드커런트	re-deu-keo-ren-teu	redcurrant
레모네이드	re-mo-ne-i-deu	lemonade
레몬	re-mon	lemon
렌즈콩	ren-jeu-kong	lentil
럼	reom	rum
리큐르	ri-kyu-reu	liqueur
사과	sa-gwa	apple
사이드 메뉴	sa-i-deu me-nyu	side dish
사냥감	sa-nyang-gam	game
사프란	sa-peu-ran	saffron
사탕	sa-tang	candy
사워크림	sa-wo-keu-rim	sour cream
새우	sae-u	shrimp
샐러드	sael-leo-deu	salad
샌드위치	saen-deu-wi-chi	sandwich
생강	saeng-gang	ginger
생과일주스	saeng-gwa-il-ju-seu	freshly squeezed juice
생선	saeng-seon	fish
살구	sal-gu	apricot

살구버섯	sal-gu-beo-seot	chanterelle
삶은	sal-meun	boiled
상어	sang-eo	shark
셀러리	sel-leo-ri	celery
설탕	seol-tang	sugar
석류	seong-nyu	pomegranate
스파게티	seu-pa-ge-ti	spaghetti
시금치	si-geum-chi	spinach
식욕	si-gyok	appetite
식용 버섯	si-gyong beo-seot	edible mushroom
신양	si-nyang	sour cherry
식초	sik-cho	vinegar
식물유	sing-mu-ryu	vegetable oil
소금	so-geum	salt
소고기	so-go-gi	beef
소스	so-seu	sauce
소시지	so-si-ji	sausage
속	sok	filling
송아지 고기	song-a-ji go-gi	veal
송어	song-eo	trout
쌀	ssal	rice
쓴	sseun	bitter
수박	su-bak	watermelon
수프	su-peu	soup
수수, 기장	su-su, gi-jang	millet
술	sul	liquors
순무	sun-mu	turnip
숟가락	sut-ga-rak	spoon
숟가락	sut-ga-rak	soup spoon
샴페인	syam-pe-in	champagne
탄산의	tan-sa-nui	carbonated
탄산 없는	tan-san neom-neun	still
탄산이 든	tan-san-i deun	sparkling
탄수화물	tan-su-hwa-mul	carbohydrates
티스푼	ti-seu-pun	teaspoon
팁	tip	tip
토끼고기	to-kki-go-gi	rabbit
토마토	to-ma-to	tomato
토마토 주스	to-ma-to ju-seu	tomato juice
통조림	tong-jo-rim	canned food
딸기	ttal-gi	strawberry
땅콩	ttang-kong	peanut
뜨거운	tteu-geo-un	hot
튀긴	twi-gin	fried
우유	u-yu	milk
와인	wa-in	wine
와인 메뉴	wa-in me-nyu	wine list
와인글라스	wa-in-geul-la-seu	glass
와플	wa-peul	waffles
완두	wan-du	pea
웨이터	we-i-teo	waiter
웨이트리스	we-i-teu-ri-seu	waitress

위스키	wi-seu-ki	whiskey
월계수잎	wol-gye-su-ip	bay leaf
월귤나무	wol-gyul-la-mu	cowberry
야생딸기	ya-saeng-ttal-gi	wild strawberry
양배추	yang-bae-chu	cabbage
양벚나무	yang-beon-na-mu	sweet cherry
양고기	yang-go-gi	lamb
양념	yang-nyeom	condiment
양파	yang-pa	onion
양상추	yang-sang-chu	lettuce
연유	yeo-nyu	condensed milk
연어	yeon-eo	salmon
요구르트	yo-gu-reu-teu	yogurt
요리	yo-ri	cuisine
요리, 코스	yo-ri, ko-seu	course, dish
요리법	yo-ri-beop	recipe
유리잔	yu-ri-jan	glass
육수	yuk-su	clear soup